SAVE YOUR

Sanity

SAVE YOUR *Sanity*
WHILE HOMESCHOOLING *High School*

Practical Principles for a Firm Foundation

Ann Karako

To my kids, who were my guinea pigs and lived to tell about it

CONTENTS

INTRODUCTION

7

1 // WHAT YOU DON'T NEED TO DO

11

2 // WHAT YOU DO NEED TO DO

26

3 // WHAT IT IS WISE TO DO

45

4 // KNOW YOUR WHY

57

5 // COLLEGE CONSIDERATIONS

68

6 // INDEPENDENT LEARNING

80

7 // SOCIALIZATION FOR TEENS

100

8 // TALKING WITH TEENS

119

CONCLUSION

135

1 // INTRODUCTION

What do you think homeschooling high school will be like? What do you WANT it to be like?

Well, I hate to burst your bubble, but it's not going to turn out either like you think it will or like you want it to.

Isn't that a lovely way to start a book? LOL. Right now you're probably wondering why you even bothered to pick it up!

Here's what I want you to know: While homeschooling high school may not proceed like what you are expecting or wanting, it can be wonderful all the same. You can have the best years of your homeschool career with your teens, even if you've been homeschooling them since they were tiny.

The key is to manage your expectations and wishes so that they can be fulfilled by reality.

"'Mrs. Lynde says, "Blessed are they who expect nothing, for they shall not be disappointed."'" --Anne, in *Anne of Green Gables*, by L. M. Montgomery

No, I'm not trying to go completely Mrs. Lynde here. (It's probably my all-time favorite book, but she is not a model to be emulated!) Rather, what we are aiming for is a level of expectations and desires that is better than none at all yet not so high that we are intimidated and scared before we start and/or are frustrated by what actually happens.

My goal in writing this book is to ease those fears and set those expectations and help you see how those wishes can come true without everyone ending up in the insane asylum. Approaching homeschooling high school with unrealistic ideas is a recipe for crashing and burning–or at least gritting your teeth a lot. Wouldn't you rather survive with your sanity intact? Maybe even enjoy the process?

Reading these pages will provide some foundational information as you head into the high school years. You'll get a basic understanding of some of the larger issues so that you can make decisions for the road ahead with your eyes wide open. I want you to have reasonable expectations so as to be able to make a realistic plan. I want to help you develop a mindset for homeschooling high school that will keep you steady through the inevitable changes that will occur as a result of all sorts of factors that you can't possibly see now, before you've even started.

If you've already been homeschooling high school for a short or long while, this book can bring you back to center and remind you of the big picture. There will still be good stuff in here to help either confirm your direction or guide you to a better one. We all need reminders as we go–I know that I sure do.

I'll be the first to admit I don't know everything about homeschooling high school. I've only done it my way, after all. There is so much out there that I have absolutely no experience with, so I don't claim to be an expert. All I can do is share from my own efforts, my successes and failures, as someone who has been around the block a few times (four, to be exact, going on five) and has some wisdom to share. I know where many of the potholes are, and I can tell you where to watch out for them. I have successfully navigated a sometimes circuitous map; I can share shortcuts and save you the hassle of unnecessary detours.

This is not a compendium of everything you need to know. I started writing that, but if I had continued, it would never have been completed!

I decided to narrow down to just setting the stage, laying some ground-work in hopes of saving you a few sleepless nights and empowering you to make decisions that are right for you, your teen, and your family.

Included in this book, then, are the topics related to homeschooling high school that I think one would most need information about in order to develop a realistic mindset before beginning–the information that will help the most towards understanding the big picture, which will in turn have the biggest impact on starting well and lasting the course. If I've missed anything, I apologize, but I think what is in this book will definitely contribute to having reasonable expectations and making good decisions that will benefit everyone in the family.

You might not agree with everything I've written. That is totally and completely ok. This book is not a directive as much as it is an encouragement. I want to build you up and give you the confidence to homeschool high school YOUR way. There is no "right" way. There is no long list of "must do's." There is a lot of freedom, and I want you to experience that.

To that end, I have also included a hefty selection of quotes from real moms who are in the trenches of homeschooling high school right now, including two "ordinary" moms who have graduated kids and agreed to tell from their perspective how it went for them. I hope these will be helpful, too, to show that everyone does things just a bit differently, and feeling "less than" or inadequate is just not necessary. You do you!

There is a resource page on my blog to accompany this book. It provides a list of all the links that you find in these pages, so you can go somewhere to click on them, rather than having to type them laboriously into your address bar each time. There will also be other pertinent information that may be helpful to supplement what we discuss in these pages. You can see it here: https://www.annieandeverything.com/save-your-sanity-resources/.

When I said earlier that homeschooling high school won't happen the way you think it will or want it to, I wasn't just being facetious. It really won't. Circumstances change, teens get attitudes, moms get tired, everyone gets hormonal–your current ideas about how this is supposed to play out most likely won't last through the many vicissitudes of life that will occur during the next few years. But that's very normal.

I'm hoping that by the end of this book you'll find a better way to think about it all. I'm hoping you'll discover freedom and flexibility and fun and fortitude. I'm hoping you'll be confident in knowing that while needs may change, you have the ability to adapt and press on. Homeschooling high school is a long-haul venture that will challenge you in many ways. I've never claimed it was easy, just that it doesn't have to be THAT hard. I'm hoping this book will strengthen you for the journey.

"When you stop expecting people to be perfect, you can like them for who they are."
— Donald Miller, *A Million Miles in a Thousand Years: What I Learned While Editing My Life*

I think the same is true of homeschooling high school. Don't expect it to be perfect. Enjoy it as it happens, for what it really is, not mourning what you wished it would be. Set your expectations realistically, based on what we discuss in these pages–and remember that the only certainty in life is change, LOL. Though it doesn't turn out the way you thought it would, it is still a worthwhile endeavor and something you can be completely proud of when you are done.

I do firmly believe that every mom can give her teen the high school education she wants for them–but sometimes our wants have to be tempered by reality and discernment in order for everyone to maintain their sanity. Am I discouraging you from aiming high or dreaming big? Of course not. This book will give you the information you need to create goals and dreams that you can actually achieve–and live to tell about it, LOL.

Let's get started.

1 // WHAT YOU DON'T NEED TO DO

Let's be real for a moment, shall we?

You know this mom: She is on top of EVERYTHING. Her house is gorgeous, she is creative, she cooks amazing meals, she LOOKS like a million bucks. She is smart as all get-out, and so are her kids.

And no matter what the question, she has the answer. She knows it ALL. (And she KNOWS she knows it all, LOL–but that's a topic for another day.) When you ask for her advice, she's gonna tell you the "right" way to do everything–which happens to coincide with how SHE'S doing every-thing, interestingly enough.

When it comes to homeschooling, she has always chosen the perfect curriculum, her kids always get all A's, they love to read, they always do their chores, they go on amazing field trips and can play a musical instru-ment like a master.

For homeschooling high school, her teens are taking Honors courses, they get AP and/or dual enrollment credit, they understand Calculus, they're volunteering in politics, and they run their own businesses. Their college applications are gonna look AMAZING.

Meanwhile, you're over here wondering if you can get by with cereal for dinner tonight again. Your teen is sullen and doesn't want to do their work. The house has an inch of dust. You're sporting the messy bun and joggers for the fourth day in a row.

AP, Honors, Dual Enrollment? Extra-curricular activities? The thought of these hangs like heavy weights on your shoulders. Life is hard enough without these things, but EVERYONE does them, right? And doesn't your kid need them to get into college?

Your conclusion is that homeschooling high school must only be for smart people who can get it all together. And since you obviously aren't that person, it's better not to do it at all.

Or maybe you started homeschooling high school with hopes of doing all these things and more–and then life happened. Money, time, money, energy, money, attitudes–some combination of these or other issues has gotten in the way of that perfect high school experience you wanted for your child. None of what you thought it would be like is happening–or if it is, it's not going well.

But you gotta push on through. MUST. DO. or your kid's life is gonna be ruined. So homeschooling becomes a HUGE burden during high school. Everyone is stressed. Relationships are worn. Family life revolves around the places the teen needs to go. What are you doing wrong???

If there is one thing I could say to ALL moms who are thinking about homeschooling high school or are in the trenches of it right now, it would be this:

You DON'T have to do ALL. THE. THINGS.

I wish I could broadcast this everywhere–over the TV and Facebook and Instagram and Pinterest and maybe a few billboards. I think so many moms would feel so much better about the whole process if they knew this BEFORE they started, or if they could find out before they get too over-whelmed.

It's easy to get caught up in the idea that homeschooling high school means following a long list of rigid requirements, of having your teen do lots o' stuff while mom organizes it all and gets the kid there and makes sure it all gets done.

What usually results, though, is that neither the kid nor the mom is happy. Everyone is stressed, in fact, because they are all pushing themselves too hard–to do things that are just NOT necessary.

One of the most important things to know during the high school years is that for the most part, you can pick and choose what you want to do. And the corollary to that is if it's not working, you can change it. The truth is that high school is almost as flexible as the earlier years, believe it or not.

Many of these things that we think are necessary? Guess what? They're so NOT.

In my Facebook group called *It's Not that Hard to Homeschool High School*, we generated a list of many of the things you DON'T have to do to homeschool high school. You might be surprised by the things that are on it (and it is not exhaustive):

1) AP courses/tests
2) Honors courses
3) dual enrollment
4) CLEP tests
5) use an "accredited" curriculum
6) pay a service to create a transcript or diploma
7) follow public school graduation requirements
8) write course descriptions
9) make your teen read specific books
10) have four credits in every core subject
11) complete every course in one year
12) get through Calculus
13) take the SAT/ACT more than once or twice (or at all)
14) be above grade level
15) have tons of extracurriculars and/or awards
16) complete more than 5-6 or so credits per year

17) be on top of life

18) spend hours each day with your student

19) know Chemistry (or any other subject)

20) never get frustrated (this is a double negative–you
   don't have to never get frustrated)

21) aim for college

22) have a career path picked out

23) get approval from extended family or friends

24) pass a GED

25) do school for x hours per day

Some of these we'll talk about in more detail in this chapter and later chapters. For now, though, take note of anything on here that you were thinking you HAD to do –and CROSS IT OFF YOUR MENTAL LIST. Or if you're uncomfortable deleting it altogether, then just move it to the side, into the column labeled "optional."

Because I am NOT saying you SHOULDN'T do any of these things.

What I AM saying is please think long and hard about what you WANT to do, what your teen WANTS to do, and what WILL work with your family life. Much of the time, when we take all of that into consideration, a lot of these (dare I say it?) over-the-top items will be stricken from our agenda.

Even for the college-bound teen. Yup.

We seem to think that because we're homeschooling, we have to do MORE in order to somehow make up for the fact that our kid has a homeschool transcript. We feel like we have to legitimize our kid's education by adding all these extras. They seem to prove from outside sources that our kid is legit, that he is worth being accepted to college because he has done all these things.

Let me reassure you right now that your homemade transcript, filled with what you have determined is a good education for your child, is sufficient for WHATEVER your kid wants to do after high school. You don't need "accreditation;" you don't need to pay someone to validate your kid's work. And you don't need to overwhelm yourself or your teen in order to impress college admissions peeps.

In my first book, called *Cure the Fear of Homeschooling High School* (which is a step-by-step handbook for research and planning so you can be sure you aren't missing anything), I share in detail how to feel confident that you are doing everything you need to do for your kid to get into college. It's pretty simple, really–just look at college admissions policies to see what they require of the high schoolers who want to apply.

When you do that, you'll discover that NONE of them require AP credits, or Honors, or even (gasp!) dual enrollment. They only specify a certain NUMBER of credits for each core subject, not the TYPE of credits–and what they do require is usually not arduous.

It's true that SOME colleges do make a big deal about how well-rounded your kid is, whether they are a stellar member of society who has their finger in every pie and leads them all. But MOST are just looking for ordinary people. You don't have to try to whip your kid into an amazing person within the four years of their high school career, LOL. There really are lotsa colleges who will be interested in your teen AS IS, lack of entrepreneurial experience and all!

Another thing you DON'T have to do? Public school requirements.

NOPE! Don't look at what the high school in your local district requires students to do; don't look at your state's education website. While this may seem like a "wise" thing to do, usually it just ends in more frustration and burn-out. Homeschooling high school is way more flexible than tying ourselves down to someone else's idea of what our teen should accomplish. (There is only one place to look for what is required of homeschoolers–but more on that in the next chapter.)

Right now I want to take some time to discuss three of the biggies that many people are intimidated by: AP courses/testing (and CLEP, which is similar in some ways), Honors courses, and dual enrollment. Each of them has pros and cons, and a discussion of these will help you decide whether you want to make the commitment to do them or not. Remember, it is YOUR choice.

AP Courses/Testing

AP stands for Advanced Placement. The idea is that the high school student will take a course that is college level, then use what they learned from that course to take a test which will prove that they learned enough to be given equivalent college credit–so that they then will not have to take that particular course (or that particular Gen Ed requirement) in college.

CLEP testing is similar, except that there is no course to take to prepare for the test. CLEP stands for College Level Examination Program. The student studies for a CLEP test on their own and takes it at a local testing site. If their score is high enough, colleges may grant them equivalent credit.

This sounds great, and for some it works well. Certainly, in the public school environment, an AP course can provide a wonderful, in-depth education for an academically-advanced student about a particular subject, and the by-product of college credit can be helpful.

For homeschoolers, though, it might not be all it's cracked up to be, IMHO.

First, there is the AP course itself. AP courses are supposed to encompass a certain level of academic rigor, and there are guidelines on the AP website. Of course, as homeschoolers we can design any type of course we want, but to give it the AP designation–recognized by colleges as having a definite meaning and needing to be approved by the College Board itself– is basically impossible. There is an approved list of courses that colleges refer to when viewing transcripts–yours won't be on there.

That isn't to say we can't create a course intended to prepare our student for the test without calling it "AP." However, this will encompass a lot of work to find resources, create and grade assignments, etc.–all without the certainty that it will really be enough to prepare the student to do well on the test. Unless you as a homeschool mom are conversant with college-level expectations for one of the 30+ subjects that are eligible for the AP designation, trying to create an AP-style course could very well be a recipe for stress and frustration.

Another option is to find an online AP class. This would be the easiest way for the homeschooler to take an AP course, and it is certainly an option. Cost may be a factor, though. When you consider the cost of the AP course plus the price to take the test, are you saving that much from the cost of the college tuition for the course? More to the point, is the cost savings worth the time and effort involved in meeting someone else's demands for scheduling, assignment requirements, etc.? This is something to weigh carefully.

And then there's the test. Just because you've gone to the trouble to craft the course or pay for an authorized one online, and your teen has slogged their way through it–perhaps with help from you–is no guarantee they will score high enough on the test to earn the credit you're seeking.

Colleges differ as to whether they will accept AP credit and what minimum score they'll consider good enough. So now you've spent the money or at the very least exerted the effort to get through this difficult course–with nothing to show for it. (The same is true for CLEP tests. Not all colleges accept them, and their score requirements vary.)

For my family, we felt this was all too much of a gamble to even attempt. Even though the buzz is that your kid will appear as the best thing to happen since sliced bread if they earn a high AP test score and that they need to "stand out from the rest"–well, we did just fine without all that. And frankly, I just didn't want to work that hard. You don't have to, either.

Plus, don't forget that AP courses and tests are designed for kids who are already academically-minded. They are not for every kid out there.

The ones who are academically inclined WILL do well in college, anyway. There will be other ways to make colleges aware of that than taking a test that may or may not pan out with the results you've been led to believe. Weigh carefully for yourself if those possible results are worth the effort to get them.

Dual Enrollment

Another way to get college credits while still in high school is to do dual enrollment. This is when you sign your teen up for a class or two at the local college, and they attend as part of their high school career. Then they are fulfilling high school requirements AND college requirements at the same time. Those college credits can then theoretically transfer to wherever they decide to go to school after graduation.

Many homeschooling families believe firmly in dual enrollment, and it is definitely a viable option. But IT IS NOT NECESSARY. Your kid can still get into college without having to prove himself first, even with a homeschool diploma. Mine did.

And while it can be very helpful to have your kid take a class from someone else, being accountable for assignments etc. to an adult other than yourself, there are cons to this, too. Consider these before you decide that dual enrollment is right for your family:

COST. While some states (Georgia, for instance) allow high school students to dual enroll for free, in many states your teen will pay just as much per course as the college students themselves–with no scholarships, hello. So where's the cost benefit of "getting it out of the way" in high school? And even in those states that provide DE for "free," the college may still charge fees which make it not so free, after all.

ENVIRONMENT. Remember, at the local college your fairly-protected homeschooler will be surrounded by young adults who are older but not necessarily wiser. These college students may converse about things you'd rather your teen not be exposed to just yet. There may be behavior on campus (public displays of affection, for example) that is uncomfortable for your teen to witness. Your teen may want to fit in and be willing to sacrifice some of your hard-fought values to make that happen. Are you ready for these possibilities?

COURSEWORK. The professor has full control over what is studied and discussed in class. Some of this may go against your beliefs or moral compass. Do you want your teen exposed to that just yet? Definitely something that each family must decide for themselves.

LOGISTICS. If your teen is not driving yet, then YOU become responsible for getting them to class three times per week—possibly with all the youngers in tow, disrupting naps or homeschool time for everyone else. Even if your teen can drive themselves, there is the length of travel and gas costs to consider, and possibly the loss of use of the car for yourself.

Can dual enrollment be a positive thing? Absolutely. But is it NECESSARY? Absolutely not. Please do not feel like you NEED to make it happen because it's the only way that you can show colleges that your homeschool education is legit. "See, my kid got an A in his dual enrollment class, so that must mean I taught him well up to that point. And it shows he's capable of college-level work." Well, maybe...

Again, colleges differ in terms of which credits they'll accept. Those dual enrollment credits may end up not counting for anything more than high school. And when you put those grades on the student's transcript, a college that doesn't accept them for advanced credit may also not give any more credence to dual enrollment grades than they do to the grades you give.

One part of your student's application that colleges look at as super important is the one with the standardized test scores (ACT, SAT). Your money might be better spent in courses to prep for those than in dual enrollment with all of its possible downsides.

Honors Courses

This is a topic that comes up often in homeschool high school circles. For some reason, we ALL think that our kids are stellar at academics and are capable of handling "honors" level work.

But what exactly does that mean? If you do a Google search for "honors credits," you'll see that most of the results are from COLLEGES defining their honors requirements for their students. There is no definitive information about what constitutes an honors course in high school.

The general idea seems to be "more work and/or more depth."

Um, okay, but what seems to be "more work" may just be that an academically gifted kid can get through more quantity in the same time frame than an average kid can. Who is working harder?

"More depth"–well, unless you survey every curriculum out there, how do you know that what you're doing has more depth than most of them?

But let's say for a minute that your kid is the most amazing thing ever and has done so much work at so much depth that you know without a shadow of a doubt that this is an honors course. What happens then?

Unfortunately, even if you put the word "honors" next to that course on the transcript–and some believe in then weighting the grade for it, which is a whole 'nother mishmash–colleges may not really care. They know that there is no standard for the term, and what one high school English teacher may deem "honors" may be completely different than the one in the next county. The general idea of academic rigor is there, but it's not an exact science.

Let's talk about it from a practical perspective: Honors classes DO involve more work, no matter how you define them. And that's not just more work for the student, but more work for mom, hello. At the very least, if you are using pre-packaged curriculum, there is more oversight and grading. But if you are designing your own coursework, then there is just plain more effort to put it together. More time, more evaluation of resources, more designing of assignments... is it worth it?

I decided it was not. I did not want the pressure of trying to justify that something was an "honors" class. The cost/benefit analysis for our family to use the word "honors" on the transcript, when I knew that it was an "iffy" term for colleges anyway, came up as a NOPE.

Can you have honors classes in your homeschool and on your kid's transcript? OF COURSE. I'm not saying you "shouldn't" do it. I'm just saying it's NOT necessary. It's another one of those "all the things" that you don't need to be intimidated by.

Do it if it works for you. Just don't give in to intimidation from others that seem to be doing it all and even implying that you are somehow coming up short.

A lot of the advice about getting into colleges out there is about the top tier colleges, anyway. (We'll talk about that in Chapter 5.) Will your child be aiming at the highest level? Most likely not. To many (if not most) of the colleges which you will be considering for your typical teen, a homeschool transcript without any extras is just as good as one filled with all the stuffing.

How to Decide for Your Family

In general, there are several things to consider when you are thinking about doing ANYTHING in your homeschool high school, from simple daily activities to curriculum to any of the extras we've mentioned here, and anything else that you hear about:

> 1) Talk to your teen. Find out what they WANT. Don't choose anything you will have to continually be prodding them to do. There is a certain amount of leeway here, as sometimes mother does know best and the kid just has to suck it up. But try to use

that card as little as possible. Getting them to do what they already want to do is a lot easier.

2) Talk to your spouse. We don't have to make the tough decisions all by ourselves. See what your other half thinks of what you're considering. They may have insight that you haven't thought of. Or they may have a definite, strong opinion or desire that takes the burden of decision-making off of you.

3) Consider YOUR schedule, NOT your teen's. It's YOU who will have to make this work, in the overall picture. Consider your family's overall schedule. If getting the teen to the community college three times a week is doable, then fine. If it's gonna involve a lot of stress for everyone because of other activities already on the regular calendar, then maybe not.

4) Consider YOUR energy level. This is something we as moms just don't often do. We want to make it ALL happen; we don't want to deprive anyone of anything just based on our own needs, so we keep pushing–and then are constantly snapping at the fam or getting no sleep or are just plain depressed, because we have pushed ourselves to the limit. We ALL need margin. Make sure you are protecting yours as you contemplate all. the. things.

5) Consider your budget. We mentioned this already, but it comes into play no matter what aspect of homeschooling you are thinking about. If you can't afford DE or AP or whatever else, then DON'T DO IT. It's that simple. If it's a curriculum purchase, then you can probably find something less expensive that will work just as well. If it's an expensive activity (travel sports comes to mind) or tuition at the community college–then just say no. Your kid does not NEED these things. They can be nice to do, but they are NOT required. I've graduated four kids who had NOTHING extra, and they ALL got into college.

6) Consider how the family will be affected. It's interesting how

this morphs as the years go by. With my oldest, we did a lot of activities, because I didn't want her to "miss out." But it involved carting everyone else around a lot, which became wearing. With the middle kids, there wasn't much that we did outside the home. Now with the youngest as the only one left, we are doing more again–because it's just me and her being affected, for the most part. Sometimes it's okay to make everyone else adapt to what the one wants to do, and sometimes it's not. It's not a problem if the youngers don't have scheduled naps EVERY day, for instance–but it is if they NEVER have them.

7) What do YOU want to do? Yes, this can factor in. Did you have this thing in mind when you were thinking of homeschooling your kid through high school? Or did it just come up, and you're not sure what to think? Do you WANT to be driving that much? Do you WANT to have to design that honors course? While we don't want to be selfish, our wants are what makes it easier/harder to do things, as well. It's not all about the other person. I personally didn't WANT to take on the extra effort to do honors courses–so we didn't.

8) What do you feel comfortable doing? This is similar to #7 but subtly different. Sometimes we do need to be willing to go outside of our comfort zone, whether in the personality sense or the time effort sense. But our personal comfort level should be taken into consideration when we're thinking about what our high school teen will be doing during these years. If you're not comfortable with them being part of the community college atmosphere, then don't sign them up for it.

Please realize that nothing is set in stone. Do-overs can be a thing, even in high school. Or you can try something and then decide it's not gonna work and change direction, and it won't ruin your kid's life. The transcript can adapt; not everything they do has to be recorded (imagine that). There is plenty of time. It's all gonna be okay!

Just remember that Madam Super-Mom from the beginning of this chapter does NOT know everything. When you are deciding what to do (and what NOT to do) for high school, don't feel pushed into a decision based on what she does or says–or on what I say! :-) Make decisions that are best for YOUR family and YOUR teen. None of these extra things are necessary. Only ONE thing is–so onward to the next chapter to find out what I'm referring to.

"Beware the barrenness of a busy life."–Socrates

Jill:

Jill is a friend of mine from way back–somewhere between 15 - 20 years, although the details escape me, LOL. We don't live near each other anymore, but we keep in touch through Facebook. She is married to a pastor and has been homeschooling their six kids from the beginning. Two have graduated; both were accepted into college. Jill enjoys family nights and spending time with church women, and she also recently started a blog called *Excellent Wife in Training.*

We did dual enrollment for our child who was planning to attend college, to help lighten his future college semesters. I did not do DE with the child who didn't want to go to college. Also, we only did DE classes that would have the least likelihood of pushing a liberal agenda: Spanish, early American history, microeconomics etc. We were warned that English 101 and others were using the equivalent of literary porn and did not want that for our kids.

Technically my kids had honors-level study through Sonlight curriculum but not "official" AP or Honors. There are two main reasons why:

1. We had a lot of children close together and it would have been too hard to push certain kids in extra work while simultaneously keeping younger kids at their work.
2. Our primary goal in homeschooling was character and life skills.

In a way, the school part of homeschool was the secondary focus. That does not mean we did not do what needed to be done most every day–but you can't do it all, and our primary focus was preparing children for adulthood and love of God and independence and an "others" focus. What we did was to prepare them for acceptance at a private university but not for exceptional academic standing. And we are okay with that.

Angie:

Angie and I recently became friends at our local homeschool co-op. She has three sons, one of whom has graduated from their homeschool and is at college now. Her middle son is at the local public school, and the youngest is still being homeschooled, although that may change. I love that Angie has chosen the best route for each kid individually–but not based on fear, since she obviously knows what it takes to successfully homeschool high school. EVERY FAMILY MUST DECIDE FOR THEMSELVES. (Just wanted to get that in here somewhere! LOL) Angie tutors English part-time and also has a fledgling photography business. Her husband is retired.

He didn't do any AP or honors courses. He didn't officially do dual enrollment, but he took two classes at our local state university (English Comp and History) his last semester of high school. (His dad works there, so he was able to use his tuition benefit by enrolling as a non-degree-seeking student.) We counted those classes on his high school transcript too, so it was a homemade version of dual enrollment.

I don't feel like he missed out on anything by not doing AP or honors courses. The only thing that was kind of a disadvantage was that we were a little clueless when we went to the first couple of college visits. I literally didn't know what AP classes were or how he could have taken them. But it didn't affect the scholarships that were offered to him.

"When I feel I'm doing too much, I do less if I can."
–Angelina Jolie

2 // WHAT YOU DO NEED TO DO

I hear from moms all the time about how relieved they are once they realize they don't have to do all the things we discussed in the last chapter. It truly is amazing how much we pile on ourselves that is incredibly NOT necessary. Are you feeling better?

But we can't just go completely our own way, either. We don't get to decide EVERYTHING for ourselves. (Rats!) There are some things we do HAVE to do as we homeschool high school, like it or not. But the amazing thing is how much freedom we have in spite of that. In fact, rather than saying we have things (plural) we have to do, I can truly say we only have ONE thing (completely singular) that we absolutely, can't-get-around-it, must, no-exceptions, be sure to do as we homeschool our teens.

Yep, it really is possible to distill homeschooling high school down to only ONE thing that MUST be done. ONE TASK that is an absolute non-negotiable, because the consequences of not doing it could truly be disastrous. But if you do this one thing, then all the rest will fall into place fairly naturally. And you'll feel tons better about all of it. You'll feel empowered to make your own decisions, and you won't be insecure about them. Wouldn't you love to be absolutely confident? You can be.

So what is the one task you MUST do?

Everyone MUST abide by their state's homeschool laws.

"Well, that's a no-brainer," you say. "Everyone knows that. But surely that's not enough for HIGH SCHOOL!"

Well, NO, everyone does not know that. This is made clear by the questions that are posed every day in my high school Facebook group from moms who obviously need clarification about what their state homeschool law says. For instance (and I found all of these within 15 minutes of scrolling on one particular day):

"I've read online that some states have laws now that a student can replace animal dissections with virtual /online options." I can almost 100% guarantee that no homeschool law specifies how labs are to be done. This person is thinking of public school laws. (The only reason I say "almost" is because I haven't read each and every state's homeschool law. But I've heard enough about most of them to be 99.99% sure–does that count?)

"Please, can you explain what is required for volunteering for high school." NOTHING is "required" for volunteering. You can have your kid volunteer or not, as we discussed in the last chapter. If this person had become familiar with her homeschool law, she would know that.

"What is a good online high school program that's not expensive yet gives them the credits to graduate high school?" This person does not realize that SHE gets to decide which credits are required for high school. She would have phrased this question differently if she knew her homeschool law.

"How many credits are required for graduating in my state (South Carolina)? I can find the homeschool laws; I practically know them by heart, LOL... but I cannot find an actual number for credits required?" That's because there ISN'T ANY requirement of a specific number of credits. She doesn't know her law as well as she thinks she does.

We seem to think that the homeschool law doesn't really mean what it says when it comes to high school. There must be more to do, right? Actually, it is LEGALLY "enough" to know what your state homeschool law says and abide by it–with nothing added. If you do only the items required by the state homeschool law, and you don't do anything else, you can completely lawfully graduate your child.

Anything else you add to your homeschool after that is YOUR choice. You can do more, or you can totally choose not to do more. YOUR CHOICE, no guilt.

BUT. (LOL, there is always a "but" when it sounds too good to be true, right?) A quick caveat here is that following the state homeschool law is often not "enough" in terms of meeting your teen's goals. For instance, if your kid wants to go to college, you may need to add quite a bit more to their homeschooling plan than just what the state homeschool law says. (But more on that in Chapter 3.)

Homeschool laws, even for high school, are for the most part incredibly simple and doable. In this chapter, I'd like to bring home just how easy they are to follow. We'll look at two sample states, one that is quite permissive and one that is generally considered to be one of the harder ones. I'd like to prove that we don't need to get so caught up in doing all. the. things; rather, we are totally within our rights to keep high school simple and unencumbered.

I talk about this in *Cure the Fear*, but I want to also mention here that it's important for you to read the law itself, not just someone's interpretation of it. Sometimes it will be necessary to have someone explain it to you, and that's fine. But you should always compare their explanation to the actual law, because it's your responsibility to follow the law regardless of what someone else says it means. If their interpretation is off in some way, you will still be liable. Some state homeschool laws are very specific; others are very general. That's why it's important for you to know YOURS.

Look for these things in your state homeschool law:

What courses to require. Often the law does not mention specific courses but rather subject areas only. For instance, the law may tell you to teach science, but it doesn't tell you which ones. That means you could require your kid to do the "standard" (aka public school) sequence–Physical Science, Biology, Chemistry, Physics–OR you could allow them to pick which sciences they want to do, like maybe astronomy or anatomy or meteorology.

How many credits. This is two-fold; it involves how many credits of each subject and how many credits total. And many homeschool laws don't even specify this! Some will say you have to teach certain subjects every year; others will say only that you have to teach the subjects but not how frequently. This means that your teen could take one semester of that subject and be done with it, if you want. And there is very rarely a total number of credits required to graduate–the public schools do that, but the homeschool law generally does not.

Evaluation. This means how you will decide whether your child is learning or not. It can mean grades, but it doesn't have to. Some states require standardized testing every year, but most do not. And just because your state requires some sort of evaluation doesn't mean they require it in every subject. For the elementary years, I only had my kids take tests for math. That was "evaluation" according to my interpretation of the law.

Portfolio. Some states require that you keep samples of your kid's work as proof that you are actually schooling them and they are learning and growing in all the appropriate ways. Many states do NOT require them, so don't put this on yourself unless you truly need to. And it doesn't necessarily have to be a big production, either. I keep end-of-chapter tests and a sampling of written work for each subject for a couple years, and then I cull things out and only keep a sample from the beginning of the year and a sample from the end of the year. They are in a file folder with the kid's name on it. Nothing fancy!

I mean, if you like spending your time putting together a scrapbook-like portfolio, then by all means go for it. BUT IT IS NOT NECESSARY. Which is the theme of most of this book–only do what you truly HAVE to and what you WANT to. All the rest is pointless!

You know what is SUPER pointless? Going by your state's PUBLIC school law. I already mentioned this in the first chapter, but it bears repeating as many times as necessary to get it through everyone's head that this is NOT necessary nor do I even ADVISE it for homeschoolers. Just DON'T do it!!

SO MANY homeschool moms get bogged down looking at what their local school district requires or what the state education department says is necessary for public school graduation. Some are doing it because they think they have to–it's a very common assumption. Others say that they're only using it "as a guide," but in my experience this only leads to frustration and subsequent burnout. The public school graduation requirements go into very specific detail about how many credits, which courses, when to take them, etc. Even the idea of "a guide" puts a lot of pressure on you to do what is listed there rather than making decisions for yourself.

I tried this for about 15 minutes, LOL. I got so scared looking at our local district's graduation requirements that I ran to my husband and told him about them. He said some magic words: "Ann, we are homeschoolers. We don't have to meet those. WE can decide what we want our children to do for high school." I was dumbfounded — partly because who knew he had it in him? LOL — but all of a sudden I had hope again. I never looked at those silly things again. Years later all four of our graduates (to this point) have been accepted by colleges, and not a single one of those admissions departments was concerned about whether we followed the public school's list.

This makes sense when you realize that colleges are deciding about applicants from MANY states, not just one. And every state has different requirements! Colleges aren't keeping track of all that. (We'll discuss what they ARE keeping track of in Chapter 5.)

So please believe me when I say that your state HOMESCHOOL law is all that matters! Don't even LOOK at the public school requirements, if you can avoid it. Put your *Birdbox* blinders on, LOL. You don't want to die trying to follow them! :-) You'll find that in most states, the homeschool law is super easy and gives you lots of leeway.

Examples

Let's look at one as an example. How about my home state of Missouri? How convenient!

(Please be aware that what follows is NOT legal advice. I am not a lawyer, nor have I ever played one on TV, LOL! This is MY interpretation of the law, and you would be advised to evaluate it for yourself and only follow what you feel you can do in good conscience. Okay? Okay. 'Nuff said.)

This is the law I've been following it for 13 years now, ever since we moved here to Missouri from California when my oldest was 12. I want to show you how you can take what is said in the law and understand how it can apply to you. You'll find that it's not rocket science! Just a little common sense is all that is needed.

Again, remember that this is my interpretation of the law for the state of Missouri only. Your state homeschool law may be completely different. I'm just trying to give an example of how things are worded and how you can interpret them for yourself.

Few Graduation Requirements

Let's look at it one section at a time. Do read all the legalese that I have copied and pasted here. Take a moment and develop hypotheses about what you think it's saying. Then you can compare your thoughts to mine. Here's the first goodie:

167.042. Home school, declaration of enrollment, contents — filing with recorder of deeds or chief school officer — fee. — For the purpose of minimizing unnecessary investigations due to reports of truancy, each parent, guardian, or other person responsible for the child who causes his child to attend regularly a home school may provide to the recorder of deeds of the county where the child legally resides, or to the chief school officer of the public school district where the child legally resides, a signed, written declaration of enrollment stating their intent for the child to attend a home school within thirty days after the establishment of the home school and by September first annually thereafter. The name and age of each child attending the home school, the address and telephone number of the home school, the name of each person teaching in the home school, and the name, address and signature of each person making the declaration of enrollment shall be included in said notice. A declaration of enrollment to provide a home school shall not be cause to investigate violations of section 167.031. The recorder of deeds may charge a service cost of not more than one dollar for each notice filed.[1]

Here it's talking about whether or not you need to let the school district know if you are homeschooling by providing some sort of documentation, which is something that many people assume they have to do. The paragraph goes into detail about who to provide this to, and what information to include, and how often to file it. BUT look at the first sentence, specifically the words "may provide." It doesn't say "must provide"; it says "MAY provide." So that means you don't have to provide it, i.e., you don't have to file yearly paperwork with the government if you don't want to. You CAN, but you don't HAVE to. (And I personally don't.)

Does your state REQUIRE paperwork? Maybe it just looks like it does, like the above paragraph. They really tried to make it look like I had to file it, didn't they? Just that one word "may" makes the rest of the paragraph obsolete, really. I don't care what to provide and how often if I don't really have to do it anyway.

Next is the definition of what constitutes a homeschool:

> *(1) As used in sections 167.031 to 167.071, a "home school" is a school, whether incorporated or unincorporated, that:*
> *(a) Has as its primary purpose the provision of private or religious-based instruction;*
> *(b) Enrolls pupils between the ages of seven years and the compulsory attendance age for the district, of which no more than four are*

---

[1] http://revisor.mo.gov/main/OneSection.aspx?section=167.042&bid=8301&hl=

unrelated by affinity or consanguinity in the third degree; and
(c) Does not charge or receive consideration in the form of tuition,
fees, or other remuneration in a genuine and fair exchange for
provision of instruction.²

This is pretty straightforward. It basically means that I teach my own family, and if I do teach other people's kids, there is a limit to how many I may teach. And I can't charge anyone to do so for them. It also mentions the "compulsory attendance age" without telling me what it is. That means I have to go looking elsewhere to find that info. Let's take a second to do that. It's found towards the end of the law:

As used in sections 167.031 to 167.051, the term "compulsory atten-
dance age for the district" shall mean:
(1) Seventeen years of age for any metropolitan school district for
which the school board adopts a resolution to establish such
compulsory attendance age; provided that such resolution shall
take effect no earlier than the school year next following the school
year during which the resolution is adopted; and
(2) Seventeen years of age or having successfully completed sixteen
credits towards high school graduation in all other cases.

The school board of a metropolitan school district for which the compul-
sory attendance age is seventeen years may adopt a resolution to lower the
compulsory attendance age to sixteen years; provided that such resolution
shall take effect no earlier than the school year next following the school
year during which the resolution is adopted.

What does your state define a homeschool as? Be sure you know this and aren't doing anything outside of their definition. Also be sure you know what ages you must be providing instruction for. In this case, since we're not talking about a metropolitan school district, the compulsory age is 17 "or having successfully completed sixteen credits towards high school graduation"–so even that is flexible, depending on how many credits my child has completed. See how we have so many things we can decide for ourselves?

²http://revisor.mo.gov/main/OneSection.aspx?section=167.031&bid=8299&hl=

Now we get to the nitty-gritty:

> *(2) As evidence that a child is receiving regular instruction, the parent shall, except as otherwise provided in this subsection:*
> *(a) Maintain the following records:*
>> *a. A plan book, diary, or other written record indicating subjects taught and activities engaged in; and*
>> *b. A portfolio of samples of the child's academic work; and*
>> *c. A record of evaluations of the child's academic progress; or*
>> *d. Other written, or credible evidence equivalent to subparagraphs a., b. and c.; and*
> *(b) Offer at least one thousand hours of instruction, at least six hundred hours of which will be in reading, language arts, mathematics, social studies and science or academic courses that are related to the aforementioned subject areas and consonant with the pupil's age and ability. At least four hundred of the six hundred hours shall occur at the regular home school location.*

Let's break this down a little.

First, it tells me I do need to keep certain records as proof that we are indeed providing an education at our house. I need to keep track of what subjects we're doing and how we're learning them ("subjects taught and activities engaged in"). But it doesn't tell me I need to do that daily, or even how often to do it. I think it implies that I should be showing it in a fair amount of detail by using the words "plan book" (implies that I am making plans ahead of time and following them) and "diary" (implies that I have the option to make a note of what we've done AFTER we've actually done it, rather than planning it out ahead of time). "Or other written record" gives me permission to record this information basically however I want, as long as it's in writing. That opens up lots of possibilities–I could potentially even just write a summary after every semester or every year. See how you don't need to overburden yourself? The homeschool law is truly usually not very onerous.

It also says I need to keep a portfolio of samples of the kid's work. I've mentioned earlier that this is giving me no direction about exactly what must be included–so I just keep a few from every year from every subject, and I shove them in a file. No biggie.

"A record of evaluations of the student's progress"–does it tell me I have to keep grades? NO. Does it tell me I have to evaluate every subject? NO. Does it even tell me what type of evaluation I have to give? NO. It just says I need to have "a record," and "evaluations" is in the plural. So they're talking about more than one evaluation, over a course of time, to show that the kid is actually learning, or not learning, as the case may be.

That means I can have the kid write a paper, take a test, do a project– whatever!–and then make some sort of note about how they did. Or I can have a conversation with the student about what they're learning and then make a note of that. This is SUCH a flexible thing. It doesn't even tell me how often I have to do this. Let your conscience be your guide.

"Or other written or credible evidence"–WOW. Talk about carte blanche. This gives me the freedom to come up with other ways to satisfy the other recording "requirements," which I put in quotes because it means those other things aren't really requirements after all, if I can come up with some-thing else altogether. The OR word is a magical thing!

In regards to (b): Now it's telling me how MUCH instruction to provide, which is no less than 1000 hours, of which at least 600 must be in "academic subjects" i.e., core courses. Does it mention how much of each subject? NO. And again there is an "or" in there which gives me license to do "related" courses. So I don't have to teach every subject every year, y'all. As long as they are getting them all at some point in their homeschool career, we're good.

It also requires us to have at least 400 hours at the "homeschool loca-tion,"–in other words, at home.

The most onerous part of that whole section is keeping track of how many hours we're doing. I do this by estimating how much time each subject takes per day and then adding them up at the end of the semester. (And in the elementary/middle school years, to make up any difference, I counted free reading, which added up to LOTS of hours in our house.) Yes, this part is a pain. But considering how much leeway there is in everything else, I can live with it!

And besides, it doesn't last forever. Look at this:

(3) The requirements of subdivision (2) of this subsection shall not apply to any pupil above the age of sixteen years.

HA!! I don't need to keep ANY of these records once my kid hits 16 years old! Woot! As of this writing, that's only TWO MORE MONTHS for me! Yea, baby!

Moving on:

3. Nothing in this section shall require a private, parochial, parish or home school to include in its curriculum any concept, topic, or practice in conflict with the school's religious doctrines or to exclude from its curriculum any concept, topic, or practice consistent with the school's religious doctrines. Any other provision of the law to the contrary notwithstanding, all departments or agencies of the state of Missouri shall be prohibited from dictating through rule, regulation or other device any statewide curriculum for private, parochial, parish or home schools.

This is a beautiful paragraph. It says that in my homeschool, I'm not forced to teach anything that is against my beliefs. It also says I can feel free to teach whatever I believe to my kids without fear of reprisal. It says Missouri may not enforce a statewide curriculum on my little homeschool. This is precious to me!

Further:

4. A school year begins on the first day of July and ends on the thirtieth day of June following.

That's pretty self-explanatory. It gives me freedom to define my school year almost any way I want. We can school year-round, or we can go nine months, or we can do six weeks on and one week off. Whatever we want!

And almost last but not least:

5. The production by a parent of a daily log showing that a home school has a course of instruction which satisfies the requirements of this section or, in the case of a pupil over the age of sixteen years who attended a metropolitan school district the previous year, a written statement that the pupil is attending home school in compliance with this section shall be a defense to any prosecution under this section and to any charge or action for educational neglect brought pursuant to chapter 210.

If anyone reports us to social services and they come knocking at the door, all I have to do is show my "daily log." So maybe that's the type of record I want to keep, rather than the "planbook" or "diary" listed above. Just in case. But this isn't saying that I HAVE to keep a daily log, just that showing one will be a sufficient defense if anyone tries to say I haven't been educating my kids. That's helpful information to know!

6. As used in sections 167.031 to 167.051, the term "compulsory attendance age for the district" shall mean: (1) Seventeen years of age for any metropolitan school district for which the school board adopts a resolution to establish such compulsory attendance age; provided that such resolution shall take effect no earlier than the school year next following the school year during which the resolution is adopted; and (2) Seventeen years of age or having successfully completed sixteen credits towards high school graduation in all other cases. The school board of a metropolitan school district for which the compulsory attendance age is seventeen years may adopt a resolution to lower the compulsory attendance age to sixteen years; provided that such resolution shall take effect no earlier than the school year next following the school year during which the resolution is adopted.

7. For purposes of subsection 2 of this section as applied in subsection 6 herein, a "completed credit towards high school graduation" shall be defined as one hundred hours or more of instruction in a course.

Homeschool education enforcement and records pursuant to this section, and sections 210.167 and 211.031, shall be subject to review only by the local prosecuting attorney.

We've been over part 6 before, but I copied it again just to show its place in context. And part 7 is VERY interesting: here in Missouri, it only takes 100 hours to count as a credit! WOW! (And would you believe that I didn't ever realize that before just now, while I'm writing?? So when you think you know your law, it's worth going back to revisit it every once in awhile! I wish I'd known this earlier–it does make assigning credits to courses much easier, and it could lighten our workload significantly. Pretty exciting!)

Do you see now how what first seems like a lot of gobbledy-gook can be broken down into understandable action steps for you? And that it's not that intimidating after all? I hope I've given you courage to look at your own state's homeschool law with new eyes. Look for phrases similar to the ones here. Look for the aspects we discussed, like attendance age, record-keeping, subjects to teach, etc.

"But wait," you say. "We've only been looking at general homeschool law, not anything pertaining specifically to high school. What do we do about knowing how many credits to do, how to give a diploma, etc? This is important stuff, right? Surely there are specific laws about that!"

Here's where many people, even those who have been homeschool-ing for years, completely jump off the deep end, LOL. Even though they've known better during the elementary and middle school years, for high school they fall into the trap of thinking they have to do what the local school district does. BUT THEY DON'T.

The seemingly "general" homeschool law also applies to high school, y'all. You do NOT need to abide by anything else, including public school graduation requirements. If your homeschool law doesn't have any graduation requirements listed–and most don't–then YOU can decide what your kid needs to do to graduate. (I realize I've said this twice before in this book, but it's necessary in order to combat this very pervasive misunderstanding. I'll probably say it a few more times before we're done!)

In *Cure the Fear* I walk you step by step through the process of determining what you think your kid should do in order to graduate. Suffice it to say here that in most states there are little to no guidelines about what must be done to earn a homeschool diploma. The law from Missouri that we went through step-by-step up above didn't require anything more than completing 16 credits!

This makes homeschooling high school so much easier than everyone believes, because you don't have to abide by someone else's rules or expectations. You can design a high school curriculum that fits your teen and your family. You can make it doable.

Specific Graduation Requirements

But just for kicks and giggles, I'd like to take a look at one of the states that DOES have graduation requirements for homeschoolers, so we can understand the difference between a law that does have requirements and one that doesn't. (And by the way, there literally are only a handful of states that do. And it truly is fairly obvious, as you'll see. So if after reading your state's law, you are unsure of whether there are graduation requirements or not–there probably aren't.)

Here is an excerpt from the text of the homeschool law for Pennsylvania, where I grew up:

The following minimum courses in grades 9 through 12 are established as a minimum requirement for graduation in a home education program:

(1) Four years of English.

(2) Three years of mathematics.

(3) Three years of science.
(4) Three years of social studies.
(5) Two years of arts and humanities.
24 P.S. § 1327.1(d)[3]

So do you see how clearly it states that these represent a "minimum requirement for graduation in a home education program"? It couldn't be clearer. They are not talking about public school here, they are talking about homeschooling, and they have a specific list of credits in specific subjects that must be taken.

Notice, too, how basic this is. They don't mention any particular courses, just how many credits in each subject. And they don't mention elective credits AT ALL. So you still have tons of leeway in how you meet these.

Are you convinced yet that homeschooling high school does NOT have to be difficult or burdensome?

As a bonus, let's look at another state that has graduation require-ments: New York. Here's the pertinent section of their homeschool law:

(e) Required courses.

(1) For purposes of this subdivision, a unit means six thousand four hundred eighty (6,480) minutes of instruction per school year.

(2) Instruction in the following subjects shall be required:
(i) For grades one through six: arithmetic, reading, spelling, writing, the English language, geography, United States history, science, health education, music, visual arts, physical education, bilingual education and/or English as a second language where the need is indicated.

3https://pahomeschoollaw.com/basic-graduation-requirements-pennsylvania-homeschool-law/

(ii) For grades seven and eight: English (two units); history and geography (two units); science (two units); mathematics (two units); physical education (on a regular basis); health education (on a regular basis); art (one-half unit); music (one-half unit); practical arts (on a regular basis) and library skills (on a regular basis). The units required herein are cumulative requirements for both grades seven and eight.

(iii) The following courses shall be taught at least once during the first eight grades: United States history, New York State history, and the Constitutions of the United States and New York State.

(iv) For grades nine through twelve: English (four units); social studies (four units) which includes one unit of American history, one-half unit in participation in government, and one-half unit economics; mathematics (two units); science (two units); art and/or music (one unit); health education (one-half unit); physical educa tion (two units); and three units of electives. The units required herein are cumulative requirements for grades nine through twelve.

(v) Education Law sections 801, 804, 806, and 808 also require the following subjects to be covered during grades kindergarten through twelve:
    (a) Patriotism and citizenship;
    (b) health education regarding alcohol, drug and tobacco misuse;
    (c) highway safety and traffic regulation, including bicycle safety;
    (d) fire and arson prevention and safety. [4]

New York is known to be one of the harder states to homeschool in, because they do have a very specific law that does list more requirements than other states, including notification in writing, creating an individu- alized education plan, quarterly reports, and annual standardized testing. Phew! So it's not surprising that they have "graduation requirements," although they don't really call them that. Instead, they just list what

[4] http://www.nyhen.org/regs.htm#e2iv

subjects need to happen during the grades 9-12. One can infer that if the kid hasn't taken these courses, they should not receive a diploma.

You can find the relevant section in (e)(2)(iv), where it discusses grades 9-12. This state is much more specific in not only how many credits of each subject they require, but also that they delineate which specific courses must be taken for social studies. But even though they require economics, for example, you still have full freedom to decide which curriculum to use for that.

One thing I find interesting in this law is (e)(2)(v), which might also be considered to be graduation requirements, since they are required during kindergarten THROUGH grade 12. To me that sounds like they must be taught every year, in contrast to other places in the law that say certain things must be taught "at least once." (But I'm freely admitting that this section isn't super clear, so don't take my word for it if you live in NY. Find out for sure from someone with more experience with your law than I have.)

But notice it says that these things must be "covered." That is a very flexible word, y'all. From my non-lawyer perspective, that tells me that we can discuss them on one day for 15 minutes and they will have been "covered." Your conscience might tell you to do a little more with them than that, which is totally fine—but you don't HAVE to. You just have to "cover" these topics, in any way you see fit. You can do whatever is easiest for you and then check the box and call it good!

Also interesting, with my newfound understanding of Missouri requiring only 100 hours per credit, is New York's definition of a unit–6480 minutes. If you do the math that's 108 hours. That's all! Easy peasy!

So now we've analyzed two states that DO have graduation requirements for homeschoolers–i.e., what a homeschooled student MUST take in high school in order to qualify to graduate and be given a diploma. And yet we've seen that even those requirements are still not all that difficult, and there is actually much freedom to choose how you want to accomplish them.

So why do people make such heavy weather of all of this? I don't know, but that's what I'm here for, LOL. I won't ever hesitate to remind you that the ONLY thing you HAVE to do when homeschooling high school is to follow your state's homeschool laws. And while each state is different and some are more specific than others, there is still SO MUCH FREEDOM to do almost whatever you want.

Now, do I think that means you can play all day and always do only what you want, as long as you meet the minimum requirements of the homeschool law?

Theoretically, yes–but in reality? NO.

There are definitely some things that are not covered in most homeschool laws that I think are WISE for you to do when you homeschool high school. What are they? Read the next chapter to find out!

P.S. This is my CYA (or maybe CMA? LOL) reminder at the end of this chapter that what I have written is NOT legal advice, and you cannot sue me if you take it as such and then find yourself in trouble thereby. You truly must study your own state's homeschool law for yourself. Also, a great resource organization of people who really are lawyers and can be relied upon for actual legal advice is the Homeschool Legal Defense Association. If you have questions about how to interpret your state's homeschool law, my recommendation is to join their organization and ask them. :-)

Jill:

I am happy with Florida homeschool laws. The state leaves the standard of graduation entirely up to the parent. What we did for high school was dependent on whether my child wanted to go to a particular college or not. It was easy to prove homeschool status to attend Florida state dual enrollment classes as well.

Angie:

The laws in Missouri appear restrictive, but they are not subject to any oversight. For that reason, parents have as much freedom to determine how their child's high school education looks as they did in elementary school.

However, parents need to understand their homeschooled children will be competing for scholarships, college admission, and jobs with public schooled children. I knew my son needed and wanted to attend college, so that was the path we followed in planning his high school education.

No, I didn't find the laws onerous. If I had a child who struggled in the core subjects, I might find them difficult to follow. But homeschoolers tend to be good at finding a different angle or method that will work for their student.

3 // WHAT IT IS WISE TO DO

Wisdom is the ability to use your experience and knowledge in order to make sensible decisions or judgments.[1]

So we've looked at what you DON'T have to do and then at what you MUST do—all of which makes it sound like this high school thing will be a piece of cake, right? If we don't have to do anything we don't want to and our state's homeschool laws are super flexible, then we can just cruise through this high school thing and give our kid a diploma, right?

Well, that would not be what I would advise, LOL.

In all honesty and integrity, I must take some time to explain what it would be wise to do, even if you don't HAVE to. I know that as parents we all want what is best for our kids, and that includes a good education. We aren't attempting this scary thing called homeschooling high school just so we can have the freedom to sleep in and eat bonbons all day. We're doing it because we think it is the best thing for our teen and for our family. And we want it to be thorough and sufficient, and we don't truly desire to be flakes. And part of maintaining our sanity is keeping our consciences clean from concern that we are doing a disservice to our kid or not being responsible about their education.

So somewhere between the extremes of doing nothing and doing everything, it is wise to live in the realm of the happy medium, where we do enough to accomplish our goals but not enough to stress us all out. As

[1] https://www.collinsdictionary.com/us/dictionary/english/wisdom

the definition above states, we want to take what we now know about what we must do to homeschool high school (and what we don't have to do) and make sensible decisions with that information. There is some solid work involved on our part, even maybe stuff we don't truly like or enjoy but still believe it's important to do. That's what we'll be talking about in this chapter.

Goals

Perhaps the most important thing I want to emphasize as something not theoretically or legally necessary but still very very wise to do is to consider your goals for your kid, and your kid's goals for their life (as much as they know them at this point, LOL). Then set up your high school so you can meet those goals.

I go into a lot more detail about planning coursework in *Cure the Fear*. But here I just want to say that even though your state's homeschool law might be super loose and have very few actual requirements, usually you will want to do more than its minimum so that you can prepare your teen for whatever is coming next.

For instance, the college your kid wants to attend may have more diffi-cult requirements for admission than your state's homeschool law dictates. So that means you will want to put the college's requirements into your plan–even though you technically don't HAVE to in order to fulfill the law–so that your kid doesn't fall short when it comes time to apply.

Or if your teen wants to start their own business, then it would be wise to incorporate coursework in entrepreneurship, such as marketing or economics–even though your state law doesn't specify those.

You see what I'm aiming for here? Don't ONLY use the state homes-chool law as your guide for what your kid MUST do during high school. What the law says your kid must do and what YOU say your kid must do can be two different things. Be wise and plan ahead for them to meet their goals for what they want to do AFTER high school.

Just don't stress about how you do that. If dual enrollment, for example, helps you fulfill those goals, and it meets all the considerations we already talked about, then give it a try! If the idea of it overwhelms you and there are other ways to accomplish the goal, then don't do it. It's that simple.

How to find out what is needed to accomplish your kid's goals? If college is the desire, then go onto college websites and find out what they require of their applicants. Colleges often have a specific list of how many high school math credits are needed, how many history, etc. In *Cure the Fear* there is a video that walks you through exactly how to do this. If trade school is the target, then they no doubt have a website, too, with the information you need.

Or call the school. What a concept in this day and age, LOL–to actually pick up the phone and ask questions! Who does that anymore? But it's super helpful and can ease many of your worries to hear a flesh-and-blood person telling you exactly what needs to be done for your kid to start their program.

Once you have this information, you can work backwards to decide exactly which courses your teen should take during high school and when. In *Cure the Fear* I provide more information about this as well as colorful, fill-in worksheets for every step of this process.

Doing this will help you feel confident that your kid won't be missing anything important that they need to fulfill their desired career/education goals. Even if they're not exactly sure what they are aiming for, you can still research various options and try to meet as many of those requirements as you can. The peace of mind this brings is worth the effort on the front end; believe me!

Grades

Another wise thing to do during the high school years: keep up with the grading. Don't let yourself slack too much or for too long in this area. Why? Because there is such a thing as a transcript coming down the pike, and it is a BEAR if you wait until the week before you need one to start grading your kid's work. Even if your state doesn't require that you grade every subject, or that you submit anything to them at all, it is wise to stay on top of this admittedly yucky task as you go. (This falls into the category of one of those things you don't WANT to do but still probably should. Sigh.)

Let's talk for a minute about grading vs. non-grading in high school. I have a personal opinion about this topic, which I'll share here. Obviously, there are other ways to look at this, and everyone must decide for themselves how to handle it. But here's what I think:

I think that before the high school years, giving grades is very much NOT necessary (unless your homeschool law mandates it). I think during K-8 it is enough that your kid is learning and progressing without having to document a percentage or letter grade. You can tell they are learning by how their writing is improving or whether or not they can divide more easily because they know their multiplication tables better than they did last year or what they have to say when you discuss the Revolutionary War with them.

But in high school, I think it's time to start grading their work.

That means that in math, I think they should have tests that cover a chapter and that you should check their answers and calculate the percentage that they got right.

In language arts, their papers should be evaluated for grammar, structure, creativity, etc. and assigned a number or letter grade based on an objective rubric.

In history, they should either be taking tests or writing papers or doing projects or all three, with definite due dates, and these should be evaluated in some way.

I think for all of these, there can be a chance to "do over," but that should not result in full credit but only some partial amount of their score given back. And there should be a limited amount of do-overs per assignment–as in ONE chance. Not as many times as it takes to fully, completely, beyond-a-shadow-of-a-doubt understand every topic on the assignment.

Then at the end of the semester, all of these grades should be averaged to create a semester grade–and at the end of the year, the semester grades should be averaged to create a final grade. And if that's a B-, so be it.

I know there are a lot of parents out there who don't believe in grading, but I think that becomes problematic during the high school years. I think you're setting yourself up for MORE work when you don't grade, because now you have to prove to colleges that your kid is capable of producing academically in some other way. This might involve writing course descriptions or compiling an official portfolio of very detailed documentation of what was done over the duration of four years–all with no idea of how it will be received by the college of choice, whose standard procedure is to look at a transcript and a GPA to decide an applicant's fate. You're basically asking the college to make an exception for your child–and while as home-schoolers we may break the norm for our kid's education, the college application process is one place where we might prefer just to fit in, ya know?

I also know there are a lot of parents out there who believe in letting their kid do work over and over until they get an A. It's called "learning to mastery," and it sounds like such a good idea until you look at some of the ramifications.

1) You are not teaching your child about ultimate deadlines such as they will find in the real world. You are implying that it is okay to do so-so work the first time, because they will always have as many chances as they need to get it right.

2) You are not teaching your child the art of studying for a test, because you'll just give it to them again. Even if you give a different test, there is still not the urgency to study and memorize and rehearse the information such as there would be with a grade that will stand regardless of how poor it is.

3) You are not teaching your child how to recover from a setback such as a poor grade would be. That D they got on that one quiz is NOT in the back of their mind prompting them to study harder the next time so they can offset it with a better grade. They have no reason to kick it into higher gear, so to speak; they can just keep cruising at whatever level they want, because it will always be sufficient.

4) You are not preparing them for the college environment where it is generally not a thing to retake or resubmit.

5) You are not teaching them to keep moving in spite of a lack of perfection, which is sometimes very necessary in the outside world. Some times we just gotta let that thing go and keep pressing forward.

My personal opinion is that all A's on a homeschool transcript isn't REAL. It's just "proof" that homeschoolers are coddling their kids and not evaluating them objectively. Very few kids in public schools get all A's– even the academically gifted ones. Is your kid truly academically gifted? Are those A's also corroborated by a correspondingly high ACT or SAT score? These are things to think about.

Also, while those A's may earn your kid admission into a higher tier college (although without corresponding test scores, probably not), will your kid be able to succeed there? Or are you just setting them up for fail-ure by having them "work until mastery" while they were with you?

If as homeschoolers we truly want what's best for our kids, I firmly believe that means that in high school we hold them accountable for their work the first time, and we record the grades that they earn.

And frankly, this does make homeschooling high school easier in the sense that we don't have to keep hammering on the same topic forever. We can move on. And our kid's transcript will accurately reflect who he is, rather than who we want him to be.

If you do want there to be some standard of learning before moving forward, then my advice is just don't set it at an A. I personally think an 80 overall grade is good enough to keep on truckin' without reviewing. If one test falls below that, as long as the overall grade is still above, then no need to redo that test. If the next test also falls below that, then there's your signal that it's time to backtrack and shore up before going on.

Do you see how much easier this becomes? Yes, homeschooling is great because you can take as much time as you want to before continuing—but don't let that become a burden. Set your standards at a realistic level, so that you can keep moving without becoming bogged down or stressed out. An A is not the be-all and end-all, y'all. :-)

Please don't throw this book against the wall and refuse to pick it up again because you disagree with me on this subject. I've got lots more to share that you won't want to miss. We can agree to disagree on this one, if you like. :-)

Standardized College Entrance Exams

Another wise thing to do, which may go against the grain for some, is to have your kid take the usual college entrance exams, i.e. the ACT and/or SAT. Whether or not you agree with standardized testing, the fact is that these are a very large part of what colleges look at to determine whether or not they will accept your student into their school.

In fact, as is mentioned in chapter 5, these scores are also perhaps the biggest thing (sometimes the ONLY thing) that colleges use to determine how much scholarship money to offer for academic scholarships. I know this is crazy and that these scores are not indicative of the whole person—I do totally get that. But this is the reality of the situation, and sometimes we have to live with stuff like this—to set aside our legitimate criticisms about it and try our best to work the existing system.

So what does that mean, practically speaking? That means you make sure to register your kid for these tests and get them to the testing center on time. The tests do cost money, so plan ahead for that and do the research about how much and when and how to register before you actually need to do it. I have a blog post with all of this information, which I've linked to on the resource page for this book.

Frankly, it is also a wise thing to make your kid take them more than once. In my opinion it is best for teens to take them to at least twice, and maybe even more.

Did you notice I said "make" your kid take it more than once? I don't often advise pulling the mom card, but in this case I totally do, LOL. Your teen, if they are like most, will hate these tests. If they don't use the "hate" word, they will for sure NOT use the "love" word. This is an experience that will be taxing, even if they are the smartest kid in the world. It involves getting up super early and crunching lotsa numbers and reading lotsa excerpts with multisyllabic vocabulary words in them. Just so not fun.

Here's the thing, though: Since we are homeschoolers, in most cases our kids are not used to taking standardized tests as much as the kids in public school are. And that first time taking a four-hour long test can be overwhelming and exhausting, and they can feel like they had no clue what they were doing. Do you really think they will get their best score? Probably not.

True story: My eldest daughter refused to take the ACT a second time, and I bowed to her wishes. We found out later that even a point or two better would have made THOUSANDS of dollars difference on her scholarship award. Can you say: "wish we'd done that differently??" After her, they all took it twice regardless of any hissy fits pitched, LOL. And my final child will take it probably three or four times, now that we know what we know and have seen it played out with her four older siblings.

So don't wait to learn these things for yourself the hard way; learn them from me the easy way!

Another thing we learned along the way about the college entrance exams that I want to pass on as something wise to do with your own kids is to have them study to take them. Don't just send them into the testing center on the day of the test with no advanced preparation on what to expect. Set them up to succeed by providing a way for them to learn how to take the test.

There are many ways to do this. With some of my kids, we used some hand-me-down books such as *The ACT for Dummies.* Nothing high-brow for us, LOL! I assigned so many pages per day over the course of a semester, and I called it "Test Preparation" and they earned .5 credit for it. Towards the end of the semester they began taking sample tests, so that they had completed several before they actually went on test day. This gave them more confidence as they were walking in there, so that they were less likely to get rattled at the new situation and were able to do their best.

My son took an online SAT Math prep course from Mr. D. (link on resource page on my blog). In this class, he had the opportunity to learn what types of problems would be on the test and how to solve them. A key component, though, was that he learned the tricks involved to move through the test quickly, without necessarily having to fully solve every problem. This was super helpful for him.

My youngest will be taking an ACT prep class at our co-op. If one of these is offered anywhere near you, I would highly suggest signing your kid up for it. There are tips and tricks that help make the whole thing easier and less stressful for the test-taker, and often it's easier to see these in action, demonstrated by an expert, than it is to read about them in a book.

As you register for the test, you can choose a number of colleges that will receive the scores at the same time you do. If you choose them before testing, the agency will send the reports to the colleges for free, so that is an advantage. It may seem scary to send them to colleges before you know what they are, but colleges do understand that your kid will probably take the test more than once, and often they will only keep the highest. Or, if they look at them all, they are comparing how your kid improved from one to the next, and they are fully capable of understanding that it's possible your kid had a bad day for one of them.

The alternative is to wait until you get them back, then go onto the testing agency's website and choose colleges to send them to. But this time it will cost you money for each college you choose. This can add up quickly. But if that's what you prefer, then just plan ahead for that expense.

What if your kid isn't headed to college? Why bog yourself down by having them take these tests? There are good reasons why I think it is wise for ALL high school students to take these tests.

First, the results can validate your homeschooling. Are you worried that your kid isn't learning anything? Then these tests will either prove that to you (ouch) or you will find out that they have in fact come away with some knowledge–which is the more likely case. They may not score very high at all, but you will know for sure that they are in fact progressing and learning.

Realize that the average ACT score is a 20. So anything above that is great, and even if they are below that, they are most likely still within an acceptable range. Which means that you can feel good about what you're doing with them and with the progress that they are making. In other words, homeschooling them is working! All those doubts you had can be put to rest. It's a good feeling.

Also, taking the test can help you identify your teen's strengths and weaknesses. Even if they don't want to go to college, finding out where they do better and where they struggle can be a starting point for discerning what they DO want to pursue. And you'll be able to start working harder on those areas that need it, because now you have objective feedback about what they are.

Not to mention that it's just one of those experiences that everyone should get at one time or another, and this is a perfect time to do it. Yes, it's totally optional, and maybe they won't ever see anything like it again–but maybe they will. Maybe at the workplace, they will be placed in a timed testing situation with bubbles to fill in. Who knows? Then having been through it at least once before, they will know better what to expect and won't be quite as intimidated.

And here's a funny thing: Often kids who have no interest in college during high school discover a few years later that attending college is the means to achieving a new goal. They become motivated in a way they never were before–and they will need those test scores for the application process. It's crazy how often that happens, and in that case, you won't want anything to be made more difficult for them by not having a score of some sort to turn in. The alternative is for the now-young-adult to take them at some point possibly long after graduation, when they haven't been working with Algebra on a daily basis–not a good idea, am I right?

We've now looked at three things that I recommend all homeschool high school parents do, even though they are not required by most state homeschool laws. The sleep-at-night factor is greatly improved when you make sure your teen is prepared for their goals, when you've graded their work to show a level of progress and understanding, and when you've gotten those annoying standardized tests out of the way. You'll KNOW you've done your job. There is a lot to be said for that.

This is not an exhaustive list, however. Every family will add more things to the "wise to do" list as befits their own particular situation. The remainder of this book will discuss more possibilities, hopefully in a way that does not overwhelm but rather helps you maintain your sanity. As always, determine what works best for YOU, for YOUR teen, and for YOUR family. Remember, there is no "right" way to do this homeschool high school thing!

Jill:

We only gave our kids grades on their transcript and in math. Here's why:

1. We wanted them to pursue doing what's right and your best because that's what God calls you to.
2. We also wanted them to seek to love to learn.
3. If they did poorly they redid it.
4. I didn't require a lot of busywork or tests. I sought that they know and embrace what they were called to learn, not to seek a certain grade for reading and absorbing.

I bought doorstopper (HUGE) books for SAT and ACT and sent the kids to Khan academy for practice. They did well enough on the first try that we did not retake. They got 1110 and 1080 and their university required 1020. They each got what I expected. He was higher in math. She was higher in reading.

Angie:

I rarely assigned grades to material, but I did assign grades on the final transcript. My basis for most of those grades was mastery. This is a model many public schools follow as well. The student might do poorly on an initial exam or paper, but they have the opportunity to continue learning the material and improve their grade.

I knew the ACT was a potential route to good scholarships, and that is something I stress to all my kids. My son completed a semester-long ACT prep class at our co-op. His teacher taught the class with a prep book by Chad Cargill. On his own, he also went through a math prep book by Richard F. Corn. My son got the score he needed for good scholarships after taking the ACT twice. I tell my kids often that they are blessed by God with opportunity and ability, and it is up to them to use it wisely and not take too much credit for it.

4 // KNOW YOUR WHY

We've discussed things you don't have to do to homeschool high school, things you do have to do, and things it is wise to do. But we maybe should have discussed something else first: WHY you're doing this in the first place. If you don't know WHY you're homeschooling high school, you can expect a lot of frustration and confusion as you attempt to do it.

> If you don't know where you are going, you'll end up someplace else."
> –Yogi Berra

If you've been homeschooling through the elementary and middle school years, you may already have this pinned down a bit, but let's take some time right now to ponder the differences between why you've been homeschooling up to this point and why you want to continue from 9th grade until graduation.

WHY HIGH SCHOOL? Why are you putting yourself through the stress and strain of figuring out college requirements, counting credits, making a transcript, and putting up with your obnoxious teen 24/7? (And the last one is probably the most difficult, if we're being honest!)

Why aren't you sending them to the place where they do this all the time? Why aren't you freeing yourself of this burden and letting someone else take care of it?

When I put it that way, you might be wondering yourself, LOL. I'm doing that on purpose–because those are the types of thoughts you'll have later, when you're in the thick of it and it's gotten difficult for a season. While I do think homeschooling high school can be the absolute best years of your homeschool career, there are those days when you just wonder why you thought it would be a good idea. When you are feeling that it might not be worth it, and you might even start thinking of ways and means to get out of it.

That's when knowing your WHY comes in handy. And if you don't have it already thought through during a time of calm objectivity, then you might not remember it during that time of emotional frustration. This is one of those "been there, done that" scenarios that I have gone through myself that I want to protect you from, LOL.

So I think it's important that you figure this out. That you take the time to think through what your reasons for homeschooling high school are. To clarify in your head–and perhaps on paper–why you think homeschooling is the best option for your teen.

To do this, you need to delineate what will be different at your high school homeschool than an experience at a public or private school. What can your teen get from being home that they can't get elsewhere? Think about this. Below are some ideas, interspersed with real-life reasons from honest-to-goodness people in my Facebook group.

Possible WHY's

For instance, is it academics? Do you feel you can give your teen a better education? We all know that there is wasted time at a brick-and-mortar building, and teachers have to deal with large classes. Sometimes academics seems far down the list of priorities at the public school, and you know your teen can progress better with one-on-one attention and the chance to move at their own pace at home.

My son needed to be challenged academically, and he was able to start college early! He was completely bored in traditional school!

Maybe your teen has an absorbing interest that takes more time than they could give to it if they had to go to school every day. My own daughter decided at 15 that she wanted to major in violin–which is kinda late, if you're at all familiar with the music world these days. She knew she would have to practice 3-4 hours per day in order to be ready in time to apply to college. So homeschooling high school gave her that time to focus on the one thing rather than being pulled in many directions.

We homeschool high school because it allows my daughter freedom to pursue her passions.

Maybe you prefer interest-led schooling, so your teen can follow many passions, not necessarily just one. So they can design their own course load based on what they want to learn about. So they can research this and then delve deeper into that–which they couldn't do if they were stuck taking the classes their guidance counselor told them they must.

We are homeschooling through the high school years because learning should still be FUN! With homeschooling, we are free to read, watch, explore and discover our interests and talents. High school is the BEST time to homeschool!

Maybe you want your family life to remain vital and important. You don't want to farm your teen out for eight hours a day while the rest of you stay at home. It's important to you that you remain a cohesive unit, and that may get damaged if your teen is spending most of the day elsewhere.

We homeschool high school because we want to teach our child how to think, not what to think, and because it makes us much closer as a family than we were when we public schooled. And being able to vacation whenever we want isn't bad, either!

Perhaps a flexible schedule is important to you. In my home, my husband's work takes him away for several days (it used to be weeks) at a time. It has been so important to us that our kids get to spend time with him when he is home, and homeschooling has accommodated that. If we want to take the day and go to the local theme park, we can do that. If we want to watch a movie together after lunch, it's entirely possible. And then when he is gone, we buckle down on the schoolwork. Are you wanting that type of freedom during the high school years?

We are homeschooling through high school for three reasons; relationship with our child, customization of the program, and freedom of schedule.

Perhaps you have a special needs child, or one who suffers from anxiety, or one whose IQ is off the charts, and you want them to have the environment they need to thrive. Any place other than home will cookie-cutter them into a grouping that may not be a good fit. But at home what they do can be individualized to suit their uniqueness.

We are starting homeschooling this year; my son is in 9th grade. He'll finish high school as a homeschooler. We decided to homeschool because the public school system was no longer able to provide what my gifted son needed.

A very common reason for homeschooling is that one's religious or political beliefs aren't represented at the local school, or they may even be derided. For many families it is important that their teen not have to face a difficult or even sometimes hostile environment for their faith or political stance.

Or perhaps the parent wishes the teen's instruction to be faith-based, which cannot happen at the public school. And private school may be out of the range of the budget, so homeschooling becomes the only option to pursue that desire.

We are homeschooling all the way through high school to train them up in the way they ought to go, so when they are grown with families of their own, they will know the truth and not stray from it. In the end, that's all that really matters.

Then there's the atmosphere at the local school–maybe you want to protect your teen from bullying or drugs or the influence of other teens who may not have the same moral code as your family. This was one of our big reasons for homeschooling all the way from K-12. My blog post about that is listed on the resources page.

We homeschool high school because of the flexibility we can have. We are able to travel when we want, and not feel the need to be telling the public school anything, or to be asking for permission. Also, to protect my child from bullying, and any inappropriate things taught out there in the school, and other classmates. I get to pick what I teach my child, and at what age is appropriate.

We are more concerned with who our children are (character) than what they know.

Do you see that all of these are possible reasons for homeschooling high school? And you may have others. The fact is that I can't tell you why you should homeschool high school; you have to figure that out for yourself. But it's worth the time to do so. Once you've thought through how your homeschool will be a better experience for your teen than sending them outside the home each day, you'll be setting a stone that will provide a solid foundation upon which to rest the building that is your homeschool..

And while any or some combination of the above reasons might also be why you started homeschooling in the first place, it is still wise to see if those reasons will also hold up during the high school years. You may have a mix of the above reasons, or just one, or you may be focusing on something completely different. But nail it down. Don't leave it in the vague subconscious reaches of your brain. Bring it out in the open and own it.

Why do you need a WHY?

Why do I stress this? Why is it important to know your WHY? Can't you just go on your merry way and do this homeschooling high school thing without really thinking about this? After homeschooling 18+ years, the last 10 with multiple high-schoolers, I can say that this is one of the most important things you will do for the success of your homeschool. Let me explain.

1) Knowing why you are homeschooling high school will help you as you make decisions during these crazy years that are filled with all sorts of options for your teen. Curriculum choices are not the only ones affected by your WHY, although that is one of the biggest areas in which knowing your WHY can make a big difference. Unit studies? Textbooks? Dual enrollment? Do they support your WHY or hinder it?

Don't forget activities. Again, choose only those that will cause your WHY to be upheld. If your WHY is family togetherness and yet your teen is out of the house at a different activity every night of the week, then you haven't taken your WHY into consideration in choosing to do those things. And I bet you're stressed and unhappy!

2) Knowing your WHY helps you evaluate whether you are being successful in your homeschooling. We get so caught up in grades and test scores, that we often forget what our real reasons were for keeping our teens at home during these years. The fact is that the grades and test scores are not the determining factor about whether you're successful– measure your success by how well your WHY is being fulfilled. And I bet you'll decide you're doing a bang-up job.

Here's a perfect example of what I mean: *We homeschool because every child is different and has different needs. Schools teach to the masses one way. We can do better by teaching to the individual's needs, encouraging their strengths, improving their weaknesses, and celebrating their individuality.*

If this mom ever feels like she's not doing a good job, because her kids aren't scoring well or getting good grades or whatever, she can come back to this declaration right here. She can take a look at whether she is encouraging strengths, improving weaknesses, and celebrating individuality. If she is doing those things, then she is a SUCCESS!

3) One of the big reasons it's important to know your WHY, which I've already alluded to, is for when you are frustrated and ready to quit. "This is hard! Why did I think this was a good idea?? Calgon take me away!!" But then you consider whether your WHY is worth the aggravation, and most

often you are encouraged to pull up your boot straps and keep marching.

We want to spend time with our kids, we want to have leisure time, we want to have the freedom and flexibility to do what we want, when we want, and be who we want while we're doing it. We may have started out with a whole host of philosophical reasons why we would homeschool, but those are the reasons we stuck it out.

4) Here's one of my favorite reasons for knowing your WHY: so you can talk to your teens when they are asking the very common question about going to public school instead. "Listen, kid, you're gonna homeschool and you're gonna like it" is not always the best approach to take, imho. Just sayin'...

When you take the time to give respect to your teen's concerns and can explain to them all the reasons why you think it's important for them to stay home, it's not only a great relationship-building moment, but it helps them understand just a little bit. I mean, we all know that they may never fully understand, but at least they'll know that you've thought this through and are really only trying to keep their best interests in mind. That means a lot to them, even if they never show it.

Do you see how knowing your WHY for homeschooling high school can be the difference between a successful homeschool, where everyone is working towards the same goal, and an exercise in frustration, because you are never really sure what you're doing?

Your WHY is a compass that keeps you pointed in the direction in which you want to go. It keeps you from getting distracted or wasting time in pursuing things that aren't necessary to meet your goals. It provides a firm foundation on which to build. It delineates your marching orders, so that you don't have to question them later.

It's kinda like reminding yourself why you married your spouse. There are times when you think they aren't really that lovable of a person, or they are SO annoying!–and you wonder why you ever saddled yourself with them. (I've been married almost 30 years, and if you haven't ever felt this way yet, you will!) Sometimes you just gotta think back to what it was like when you were dating, and remember what it was about them that you fell in love with. Chances are they haven't changed that much, and those qualities are still there, even if they are hidden a little or circumstances have made other, lesser qualities come to the fore. When you remember these good things, then moving forward seems much more doable–and so you adapt and continue to make the marriage work.

The same thing is true of homeschooling, and especially homeschooling high school. YOUR TEEN WILL DRIVE YOU BONKERS. And you'll really really really be tempted to get rid of them for eight hours a day! But your reasoned-out WHY will bring you back to basics and help you adapt to find ways to keep things going through graduation.

So maybe some of the above reasons fit you, and maybe they don't. Even if they do, it would be wise to reword them to say exactly what YOU think. And if they don't, or you still feel like something is missing, then you might want to spend some time being more intentional to discern your own WHY for homeschooling high school.

Your Own WHY

As you do so, think about what is important to you. Here are some questions to get you started:

--What do you want a high school education to look like in your home? What do you think should be learned? How do you think it should be learned?

--What type of adult do you want your kid to be? What values do you want them to hold? What do you want them to look back on?

--What is your family identity? What makes your family different than any other, aside from genetics? What are the bonds that hold you together?

--What are the circumstances in your life? What is your budget? How busy is your family? Do you work outside the home?

Maybe there is a quote or Bible verse that you want to base your vision on. Here's an example: *We boatschool our two teens as we cruise new waters and learn from the world around us. "The world is a book, and those who do not travel read only a page." ~St. Augustine*

All of this goes into your WHY for homeschooling–teen edition. Take some time today to begin clarifying your thoughts about this. Talk it over with your spouse. Get specific. Then write it all down and save it someplace so you can pull it out and refer to it over and over again. There will be days when you need to remind yourself. There will be days when you think of something new to add.

And there will be days when you look back and say, "Yes, we did what we set out to do. Maybe it wasn't pretty all the time, maybe we took some detours or made some mistakes; but overall, we accomplished what our hearts wanted." And that's a great feeling.

The whole point of this book is to provide encouragement and information so that you can ENJOY the high school years in your homeschool. Knowing your WHY is a crucial aspect of that. You can't really relax if you have no sense of direction; instead, you flounder. And stress is the direct result of feeling out of control; but knowing your WHY gives you that control, because it is the basis from which everything flows.

Here are some more examples of real-life WHY's:

We homeschool because his future is too important to just be one in a crowd. One-on-one attention, and a goal of mastery vs "good enough." We move at his pace, whether it's fast or slow.

We homeschool for many reasons, but the one reason that stands out for me is I remember what high school was like for me. There was pressure to perform, pressure to fit in, pressure to act "normal." I want my children to feel comfortable in their own skin and with their own uniqueness. Mission Statement: I strive to raise children who are well adjusted and love God with all their heart. I want for them confidence and indepen-

dence - to be able to recognize their own strengths. I pray they value determination and hard work. I pray I create inquisitiveness and instill a lifelong love of learning.

We homeschooled through high school for the same reasons we hs'd all other grades:(1) to instill the principles of our faith and give opportunity to put our faith into action; (2) to gear the learning to the exact level of the student; (3) to adapt courses to the bent of each child; (4) to build discipline and an independent, entrepreneurial attitude.

I stuck with homeschool in high school to give my kids freedom to work at their own pace and to hybridize their schooling. They were able to choose classes at the public school part-time, which is all they wanted due to anxiety issues, online classes, and dual enrollment based on their interests and needs.

We homeschool high school because I'm confident they will receive a better education at home than they would in public high school. Too much pressure there all around. On top of this, they are able to really spend time honing in on life skills, as well as interests and passions they want to pursue in college and/or career.

I want the love of learning to stay with my boys. Home school through high school lets them explore their interests and helps them understand exactly who they are as an individual.

Take the time to figure out your own WHY for homeschooling high school. You'll be glad you did.

Setting goals is the first step in turning the invisible into the visible.
– Tony Robbins

Jill:

When the kids were little I was thrilled to have them home to school together and give them freedom in their schedule to play and be friends with their siblings. (And snuggle with me reading books).

In the high school years I was thrilled to have them home to get enough sleep, to be friends with their siblings and have the time and energy to invest in church ministry, family time and not suffer through the frequent unkindness, unwholesome speech and industrial-strength sexual hormone displays of public and private schooling.

By the time my kids reach high school our goal is for them to be independent learners, to learn to manage their time and to provide opportunities to be disciples and flourish in a positive environment where I can also see their sin and weaknesses (and strengths!) and address them on an ongoing basis.

Angie:

My son had always been homeschooled, and I had always planned to continue through high school. Of course I did reevaluate each year, but I saw no reason to put him in public school. Also, he wanted to continue homeschooling. If he had wanted to go to public school, that would have been fine.

5 // COLLEGE CONSIDERATIONS

I remember a kid from my graduating class who applied only to Ivy League schools. He wasn't at the top of the class–or even very near it–but he and his parents were certain of where they wanted him to go. Guess what? He didn't get in ANYWHERE that he applied. He had to rush to apply elsewhere at the tail end of our senior year. It's a cautionary tale– but there's no reason anything like that should happen to anyone reading this book. By the end of this chapter you'll know what you need to in order to make wise decisions concerning college for your teen.

I think one of the biggest fears people have about homeschooling high school is whether or not their kid will get into college. They are afraid they will actually hinder their kid–that their transcript won't be accepted, or that the courses they do won't be acknowledged, or that their kid won't be ready.

I consider this a foundational topic because if college is your goal– whether it be your kid's goal or your goal for your kid, and there is a subtle difference–then this is something that will color all the decisions you make as you homeschool. It will affect which curriculum you choose, which subjects/credits you require, how much independent work you expect (more on that later), etc.

Also, it's good to get some of the worries about preparing for college out of the way before moving on to other topics. Sometimes we have ideas that are just not accurate, and if we continue to live by them, we will stress ourselves unnecessarily. And who needs that? So let's focus on this now, so we can remove any burdens about it that you might be carrying.

When we think about preparing our kid for college, often the first thing we do is a Google search: "how to prep for college," "what are colleges looking for," or something similar. And what we find is a lot of advice from a lot of different people, and it usually sounds very involved and scary, and we get freaked out.

I just did a search for this again recently, and I was appalled at what was being said. It made me feel like my remaining kid has NO chance–even though I've already graduated four of them who have all been accepted at colleges. These articles can be SO intimidating!

There is a reason for this, and that is that most of the information you'll find online is aimed at people trying to get their kids into top tier-colleges. This information really doesn't reflect reality for most of us.

Remember that mom in the first chapter? It's easy to get frustrated when we see moms like her, because they are over-the-top achievers, and their kids are uber-intelligent, and so everything they do looks easy. And their kids are applying to Ivy Leagues (or something like it), and so we think that is what we should be doing, too.

Frankly, we all have a little bit of that mom in us, to be brutally honest– but you know it's true. As homeschoolers we tend to be a self-sufficient, capable bunch. And we tend to aim high in everything, including which colleges our kids will apply to. And there ain't nothin' wrong with that.

Except when it causes stress and discord and turns homeschooling into a difficult chore rather than a time to enjoy being together. Except when you find yourself doing a bunch of things you don't want to do, rather than choosing what's best for the entire family.

What we need here are two sanity-saving perspectives:

1) It is important to have a realistic view of who your kid is and what type of school they will excel at, and

2) It is helpful to realize that there are LOTS of options for colleges out there, and most of them are VERY reachable.

Let's deal first with the idea of our kids' abilities and where they will fit in.

Where is a Good Fit for Your Kid?

Here is where I step on the toes of almost every homeschool mom out there, because frankly we all think our kid is "special" or "advanced." How many homeschool moms of elementary kids are all about "well, age-wise my kid is in third grade, but he's doing 6th-grade work"? You know what I'm talking about, don't you, and you may even have been one of them.

And in elementary school our homeschooled kids do often progress faster than their public school counterparts. These are some of the beauties of homeschooling–that our kids get a one-on-one tutor 24/7, and there is no class time wasted on pointless tasks, and we can choose curriculum that works for our kid.

So our kids do learn the intricacies of addition more quickly and also probably more thoroughly. That "more thoroughly" part means that multiplication and fractions also come easier, so it's less necessary to spend as much time in review–and before you know it, our kids are far ahead of their public school counterparts or grade level standards. The same is true for reading and spelling and whatever else.

But a funny thing often happens around the early teen/middle school years. That kid that was such an overachiever hits Algebra–and everyone's world is rocked. All of a sudden the knowledge of fractions and decimals doesn't matter as much, and abstract thought becomes a thing. And the brain that we thought was so advanced turns out to be actually pretty average.

If it doesn't happen with Algebra, it may happen with Chemistry, or with reading Shakespeare or writing papers. Our "advanced" elementary kids often turn into ordinary teenagers. (And just a hint–it doesn't only happen with academics but often with behavior, too. Your model child may not be so model once they hit 13; just sayin'...!)

Some of you are chuckling right now, having been through this and having come out the other side, while others are reading this with a sense of awakening–"Oh, THAT explains it." And others don't yet believe this will really happen, because they still believe their kid is more special than the rest out there. And he may be. But probably not. :-)

The point is that we start cherishing ideas of what type of school our supposedly advanced kid will qualify for, and it can be hard to release those hopes. Because you know as well as I do that it is validating our homeschooling when we can say our kid is three grade levels above their age and then also when we can drop names like Harvard and Yale. Or at least when we think "top tier" in our minds, because we've done such a good job with our kid, and they are so bright!

Slowly those ideas begin to crumble, because reality sets in. And yet we're still holding onto a serious-college-prep track for high school–our kid is capable of it, after all, right? So we load up their plan with LOTSA core courses and honors and research papers and in-depth projects and starting a non-profit and whatever else.

What often happens, though, is that the kid no longer seems as interested in that stuff as we are. They aren't motivated to work that hard, and when they are, they still aren't getting the grades they'll need to shine above the crowd. And that ACT or SAT score? It's meh at best.

If you are the mom whose kid stays motivated and overachieving and earns the high grades without needing to re-take things five times and gets high scores on the college entrance exams, then this section of the book– actually, maybe the whole book, LOL–may not be for you.

But if your teen is suddenly seeming really pretty average and you're not sure what to do about it, then please continue reading, because we're about to take a huge load off.

And I'll just jump to the main point, because I want you to feel better RIGHT NOW. Here's what I have to say about the whole preparing for college thing:

Most kids are NOT top-tier kids. Most kids aren't even second-tier kids. Most kids are better suited to the closest state school or a small private school or junior college or even the local community college.

And listen to me, homeschool mom, when I say that these are all very viable and acceptable options and do not reflect poorly on your parenting or your homeschooling or your kid.

The colleges you should be aiming for are the ones at which your kid WILL shine above the crowd. And they are out there, because not every college expects a 32 on the ACT and a 4.0 GPA with a gazillion hours of extracurriculars and volunteering. Many colleges are happy with your average kid's average ACT score and B+ GPA and no extras. TRULY.

Do the research to find out what THOSE colleges require of their applicants and shoot for that. Don't aim so high that your kid's entire high school career is fraught with anxiety, frustration, and difficult days due to not measuring up to the rigorous plan you've set out for them.

What do we REALLY want for our kids? We want them to be well-adjusted, responsible adults. People who can be relied upon to show up at work on time and do a good job. Is the name of the school on their degree really that important? It's only a small percentage of the general population that has a degree from a top-tier college, and homeschoolers shouldn't think that we are the exception to that statistic.

And frankly, the scholarship money won't come to your kid from the upper-tier schools, anyway, most likely. The scholarship money will come to your kid from a school where your kid is in the upper level of the candidates that are applying. That means you should maybe shoot LOWER than their abilities, so they really stand out. That's the practical truth of it, and your kid will still end up with a degree–and with whatever education they want to create from where they go.

If you want to be homeschooling high school without losing your sanity, then be realistic about which college(s) you and your teen are aiming for. You'll all be much happier.

Is Your Kid a Good Fit At All?

In fact, this begs the question of whether your teen even needs to go to college at all. I know this is a radical thought among homeschool families, but it should be considered. IS YOUR KID COLLEGE MATERIAL??

We decided our second child was not, although it took us two expensive years in college to figure it out. She came back home and started working full-time instead, and she says it was the best decision of her life. I only know that we have our cheerful, spontaneous kid back again, both geographically and emotionally, and that makes me happy.

We also decided our fourth child was not college material at the time that he graduated, and he's been working and waiting until we all agree he is capable of tackling the demands of the college lifestyle and academic workload. It's getting closer, but 16 months after graduation, we are not quite there yet. And that's OK.

Maybe your kid shouldn't be trying to prepare for college AT ALL. There are SO MANY options out there, from a technical school to working full-time to an apprenticeship to entrepreneurship and about a gazillion others.

If learning ancient history just for the sake of it doesn't go over very well in high school, it won't go over well in college. And trust me when I say that's a LOT of money to spend (or to find in scholarships) when your kid is kinda meh about the whole thing anyway.

Do some career exploration with your teen, or have them do it themselves. What are their talents and strengths? Do they like words or numbers? Do they like being physically active or do they prefer something more desk-bound?

You can actually turn career exploration into a .5-credit elective by using the curriculum that I list on the resource page on the blog. It's full of links to talent inventory questionnaires, and it also makes the teen think about what they want out of life. It can really help them along the way to choosing something to do or study or work towards after high school graduation.

College doesn't have to be the end result of your teen's homeschooling years. It's not the only way to validate your decision to keep them home this whole time. A responsible adult who is considerate of others and will eventually be living independently is just as wonderful a result, believe me.

When They Don't Know Where They Fit

Here's another thought: it's okay if your kid doesn't know what they want to do or study after high school. Don't force what they aren't mentally ready for.

Sometimes I think that the obscene plethora of possible paths that exists in modern society can be a real hindrance to our kids. In the pioneer days, if your dad was a farmer, you became a farmer. Now teens have basically the entire world to choose from. How can we expect our kids to know beyond the shadow of a doubt that what they think they want to do today will be what they want to do tomorrow? Or next year? Or in ten years? In most cases, this is not realistic, either.

So then how do you homeschool high school if your kid has no clue what they want to be when they grow up?

First, you try as best as you can to cover all the possible bases. That means you do some research about what colleges require, and you build some semblance of that into your kid's coursework plan, as we discussed in Chapter 3. You don't have to go all-out, but do try to at least get the minimum going. If your kid decides halfway through senior year that college is the place for them, you want the necessary things to be in place–or most of them, anyway.

If your kid doesn't meet all the requirements at that point, there is no need to stress. Many colleges offer "remedial" courses to bring this type of kid up to the necessary level, and the students take these courses their first semester or two before they can take the actual college-level courses they need.

Or another option is to take those courses at the community college to get your kid's feet wet, so to speak, and then they will be ready for "real" college. This may take more time, but that's totally ok, because the timetable will be driven by your kid rather than by you–which means it will be right for THEM.

Second, try to allow them to explore their interests as much as possible, so that they can begin to narrow down what they like and don't like. Find curriculum that lines up with their hobbies or talents. Sometimes a one-semester course is enough for your kid to be like "nope, not really wanting to pursue that one any further." Or "YEP, let's keep going on this one."

My third child started college as an illustration major. In her first art class at the college level, she realized she didn't really like working to someone else's specifications, and that art was really better left as a hobby for her. She switched majors and is about to graduate in accounting. Kids are crazy that way, aren't they? So give them every chance to explore things in high school where it doesn't cost anyone any money, LOL.

Third, remember that there is beauty in education for its own sake. This can be a great time to cultivate a love for learning in your teen. Find great books to read and discuss, deep philosophical thoughts to pursue, lives of famous people to learn from, etc. A liberal arts education is worth something, too. You can grow the mind and heart of your child without being restricted by specific life goals.

Or use their part-time job for credit, find the minimum coursework to meet your state's homeschool laws, and call it good. THIS IS ALSO A VIABLE OPTION. Again, what is our aim? A responsible, happy, considerate adult. More is gravy.

As long as we're on the subject of college, let's talk about money. Scholarships, loans, grants–how does one make heads or tails out of them? This can be a huge source of stress during the high school years.

I'm going to give you my knowledge in this area, which is based on my experience. Obviously I don't know everything about this, and you are wise to do your own research. But if I can reduce some of your anxiety by sharing with you what we went through and what we learned from that, then so much the better..

Many homeschoolers think their kid will get a full ride to college. It's that same thing we've already talked about–our kids are special, advanced, etc, and they deserve a full scholarship, so they will get one. We just have to do enough work to qualify for one and enough research to find it in the first place.

Well, it's not that easy.

My eldest daughter and I had that same idea. If she had a good enough transcript and if she did enough leg work, we would be able to find and apply for scholarships so that if she won enough of them, she would earn a large sum of money towards her college tuition and expenses.

Unfortunately, most of the scholarships that you apply to out there are not really designed for homeschoolers. Many are based on ethnicity or what the father's job is or whether a parent is a veteran or geographic location or choice of major–none of which applied to us. Many specify that only public school kids are eligible to apply, or their requirements are such that only public school kids will meet them. We spent a long discouraging time trying to find scholarships for her to apply to, and she filled out the paper-work for a handful–and never heard back from any of them.

That doesn't mean that homeschoolers can't get scholarships. In fact, the easiest way to receive one is from the college itself, either for sports or for academics. I don't have experience in obtaining a sports scholarship yet, although we will be pursuing that route with our youngest.

I do have experience with academic scholarships, often called merit scholarships. All of my kids who were accepted to college were offered some sort of merit scholarship; these arrived in the same mail envelope as their acceptance letters. But the amount wasn't based on their transcript or their extra-curricular activities; it was solely based on their ACT or SAT scores.

Here's how I know that: My eldest received a partial scholarship and went to college. That first year she busted her buns and got a 3.9some-thing GPA. She went back into the financial aid office and asked if her scholarship could be increased. They said no, that's not how it works, that her scholarship was based on the scores she submitted when she applied and would never change, no matter how well she did in college itself.

Which means some kid who gets a high ACT score but totally goofs off in college will still get his money for all four years, as long as he maintains the GPA required by the scholarship (which is often a 2.5 or 3.0). Seems unfair, doesn't it? But these are the things to know before you start the process, so that your expectations are realistic.

Further, notice I said that she received a partial scholarship. Most schools do not just hand out full scholarships willy-nilly. If your kid gets a VERY high ACT or SAT score, you might be in the running. But many schools don't do that AT ALL, regardless of score.

My third daughter received a 31 on the ACT, which is considered to be very high. At the college she wanted to go to, she received the highest scholarship they offered–which was for HALF tuition. Sigh.

OK, so this sounds rather gloomy. You're probably wondering if there is any way at all to get a full scholarship, if colleges don't offer them with their acceptance.

Well, one thing we found out–also the hard way, LOL–is that many schools will have a scholarship competition to which they invite the higher-level applicants. This is often a day or weekend where these kids come visit the school and get interviewed, take tests, write papers, etc. The kids with the best outcomes from this competition will get offered more money than their original offer. The daughter with the half-scholarship attended one of those and was offered another $1000 per year as a result. The winner of the competition was given a completely full ride, and the second and third place finishers were also given a huge chunk of scholarship money.

But one thing to notice again is that this is first mostly based on test scores, and THEN on who the kid is and what they can do.

Which just gives more weight to the idea that there is no reason to stress yourself out trying to do all. the. things. to get your kid into college and to get college paid for. If you want to put that kind of effort into anything, put it into test prep. That's where you'll receive the best return on your investment. A difference of just a point or two from one test session to the next can mean thousands more dollars in scholarships.

The main point of this chapter is not to stress about college. Do your research, plan to meet the requirements, take the tests, and above all, apply where your kid will be a good fit. When you do these things, there is no worrying necessary. So you can relax and actually enjoy the process of homeschooling high school, making decisions based on what works rather than on meeting some pie-in-the-sky standard. Don't you like the sound of that?

"But wait," you're thinking, "although I feel better, this is still not quite enough. Just because my teen can get into college, how will I know I've prepared them to succeed there?" That, my dahling, is one of the benefits of the topic to be discussed in the next chapter. I've gotchu! :-)

Jill:

I LOVE ONLINE APPLICATIONS. Wow! So much easier than when we were students! I found it straightforward and easy and I appreciated the college checking off our list online as they received application items so we always knew right where we were.

What I didn't like was that once my kids' names were in College Board for the SAT we received 500 pieces of mail for child for every college under the sun!

Angie:

We visited three college campuses during and right after his junior year, and two of them stood out as good options. We also went to a college and career fair early in his senior year, and I wish now that we had done that in his junior year. To be able to talk to a large number of colleges in just a couple of hours is a great idea, even if most of them are not interesting to you at all. Plus we walked away with a bag full of assorted pens.

Finishing the high school transcript was stressful and intimidating, but it shouldn't have been. It was just a matter of buckling down and getting it done. I purposely kept it simple.

6 // INDEPENDENT LEARNING

In my little life, high school has actually been the easiest stage of homeschooling– and all because I was simultaneously stressed out and lazy in the younger years. What I did then just to cope turned out to be the foundation for high school years that ran mostly pretty smoothly and without much input from me.

A little bit of background: I had five kids in eight years, y'all. And we lived in a 1200 square foot house with THREE LARGE DOGS. It was cozy and crazy, and I was pretty much always stressed out. LOL. (If I had those years to do over again, based on what I know about me now, that I didn't realize then... sigh.) So my eight-year-old was homeschooling, as were her six-year-old and five-year-old sisters, and the only boy child was being as emotional and destructive and sweet as only a three-year-old can–and I was nursing a newborn. This was back in 2003–the stone age, LOL.

Back then there were no blogs or podcasts. Curriculum reviews were only found in Cathy Duffy's book or the Rainbow Resources catalog, and there was not the vast array of curriculum choices that there is now. A lot of what I was doing I had to figure out for myself, with no one to hold my hand or to get ideas from.

As is my general tendency, I tried to make everything as easy for myself as I possibly could, while at the same time getting all the stuff done. It was just NOT POSSIBLE to sit down with each kid during every individual subject; and at that age, doing subjects like math, spelling, and grammar together was just not gonna happen–the kids were too widely separated in ability and knowledge level. My little controlling self put together a very defined schedule to put me where I needed to be when the kid needed me to be there, but even that didn't solve all the issues all the time.

In desperation, one day I told the eight-year-old to read the Abeka math page and figure out how to do the problems for herself. I had other things to deal with when I was supposed to be teaching her math. And lo and behold, she did. The next day I told her to do it again. I'm not stupid; I can recognize a good thing when I see it–not to mention that it freed me up to deal with the three-year-old's temper tantrum or the baby's nap ending earlier than usual.

And thus a manner of learning that became an important pillar of my homeschool philosophy was born.

Independent learning is, in my opinion, the best way to handle the problem of kids in multiple school levels, especially when one or more is in high school. It's not only best for mom, which was totally my original motivation, LOL–but it is also best for the students. It prepares them for college in a way that teacher-led learning cannot.

I'm here right now to encourage you to go to your kid and tell them to do it by themselves, that you're not gonna do it for them anymore! Okay, well maybe not that drastic just yet–but I do totally recommend that you work towards the reality of your high schooler doing EVERYTHING without you. It IS possible, and it IS a good thing. And it solves the problem of you having to be everywhere at once, which is something all homeschool moms deal with to one degree or another.

For our purposes, I define independent learning as the process in which your kid is reading the text or watching the video or somehow receiving the instruction/content for each lesson, then doing the corresponding assignment(s), then correcting their own work and learning from their mistakes, then turning in to you a finished paper or a completed chapter test or some other culminating project for grading. You are around to answer questions, but you are not hands-on day-in and day-out. You don't deal with the daily work; they do. You only deal with the bigger things, and then only as the grader, not as the I'll-help-you-do-this person.

Aren't you thinking right now that this would be pure heaven? It's totally possible. But just in case you're someone who hasn't been convinced yet, let's discuss the benefits of independent learning. There are many of them.

Benefits of Independent Learning

1) Obviously, as already mentioned, there are benefits to mom when this is happening. She doesn't have to sit down with each and every student for each and every subject. She is not stuck in the homeschool room all day (or in my case, to the homeschool dining room table). She can get chores done around the house, nurse the baby, use the restroom (what a concept)–all while school is progressing merrily along.

2) The benefits in a large family are also obvious. Even when you do several subjects as a group, it is still difficult for mom to individually teach every child. No one lady should have to be stretched that thin or have to create that many lesson plans. Large family homeschool dynamics almost force one to embrace independent learning with a vengeance!

But mom isn't the only one who benefits. And frankly, the benefits to the kids are why we continued using independent learning and even fostered it more and more as the kids got older. I began to see what they were gaining from this practice, and it has paid off in a big way.

1) The child learns how to read (or listen) for understanding. This is a skill that takes practice, and it is a biggie on standardized tests. When the child is answering questions based on what they have read (or watched or heard), it is a way of holding them accountable. They will learn to concentrate as they read (or watch or hear), because they will know they are going to need to use the information for their homework.

This also facilitates the skill of note-taking. If they know they will need to know it, they will be more motivated to jot things down as they read (or watch or listen). Note-taking doesn't have to be this major skill that you teach from the ground up; often your kid can figure out their own way to record what they're learning. For a while you can sit down with them and model the practice, if you like. But you don't have to worry that they are doing it wrong if they do it differently than you. A major concept we all have to get over is this assumption that our kids learn like we do and need to have material presented and archived like we do. NOPE. Let them figure out how they work best.

2) The child learns HOW TO LEARN. This is HUGE. When a child has become accustomed to learning independently, they can pick up any book and learn the information in it. This means they can continue a lifestyle of learning throughout adulthood. They will never be dependent on someone else to teach them something.

Isn't this what we want for our children? To become lifelong learners? When they know how to teach themselves math and grammar and history in school, then they can transfer that skill to just about anything else in life.

How to cook? Follow the recipe. Look up the words you don't know, like sauté or braise.

How to know if that weird noise in your car's engine is something to be concerned about? Sure, Google it–and then figure out what the mechanic dudes are saying in the forums by asking more questions or buying the maintenance manual for your make and model. Then you can learn how to change the oil for yourself or give it a tune-up.

Worried about the state of the nation? Start reading about our government, about the political parties, about how laws are made, about economics, world trade, etc. etc. etc. Then you can begin participating in local politics to make a change.

Want that promotion at work? Find the boss and ask them what you need to know first–and then do what it takes to learn it.

Each of these types of situations start by being confident that you can learn what you need to learn. And that confidence comes from having done it already, in the safe environment of the homeschool. Especially the high school homeschool, because hey, if you can teach yourself chemistry, you can teach yourself ANYTHING.

3) The child has greater freedom to determine their own routine. When mom is not part of the equation for learning a particular subject, the child can schedule that subject any time in their day. This often helps with motivation and effort. There is nothing worse than being ready to do the next history lesson but having to wait for mom to be available. Well, with independent learning the kid can just go ahead and do it whenever they want.

4) The child learns about their own learning style. This is also HUGE. When mom is in control of their entire day, the kid doesn't have the opportunity to experiment with different environments, times of day, or methods of learning. As mentioned above, we tend to think they will learn the way we do. Guess what? They are different individuals, and when we try to fit them into our mold, sometimes lotsa frustration can ensue.

A good pointer here is to think about how your spouse learns, and see if your kid matches them more than you. I like to read and see what I am learning about; my husband prefers to listen. I want to show him something; he wants me to tell him or read it to him. It was a light-bulb moment when I realized our #2 was the exact same as him. DUH.

When we give the child room to experiment by having them learn on their own, they become more self-aware, discovering how they like to learn, how they learn best, and how they do not. That might be with earbuds in, or lying on the floor, or late at night–all those things we think are "bad." Well, for that kid, they might actually be "best." But they'll never figure that out if we don't let them do some trial-and-error. Independent learning allows that to happen.

5) The child is free to learn at a faster pace. If the child is capable of understanding something well and wants to keep going, he can. He is not held back by mom's lesson planning or availability.

A large part of why we want to homeschool is because the classes at the public school progress so slowly, sometimes. Or too fast! Either way, why do we want to force our kid to learn at the pace that WE set? Sometimes, obviously, they might need to be prodded along if they're not being diligent; but when it comes to how quickly they learn, independent learning allows them to go at the pace that suits them. And many times that means they're cruising ahead when we would still be trying to determine how many pages they needed to read this week and would have told them for the 10th time that we're too busy to teach them factoring right now.

6) The child learns perseverance and self-reliance. This is another really wonderful benefit of independent learning. It can be tough to stand by and watch while your child works through a difficult problem. We often want to jump in and help them. But if they are in charge of their own learning, then they have the chance to prove to themselves that they can figure it out without us, which is part of the growing-up process. It helps ensure that they won't still be living with us when they're 30, LOL.

When they struggle through to success, they have learned a very valuable lesson. Some things don't come easily, but by not giving up, success is possible.

Does this mean they can never ask questions? Of course not. We are there to help as needed. But even knowing when they truly need to ask a question for help versus when they could really press on without it is something they will learn here. Which leads us to the next point:

7) The child learns initiative. The responsibility for learning is ON THE CHILD. He needs to do everything he can to find the answers he needs before asking mom for help. This may mean going back and reviewing previous material. (This is a good habit and also helps with studying for tests.) Or it may mean looking for outside sources of assistance — even looking a word up in the dictionary, gasp! Or it may mean going to the answer key and working backwards. This is perfectly acceptable, mom!! Once the kid sees how the problem was done, they can then apply that to the next problems. Sometimes you do need to know the end result before

you can figure out how to get there.

My eldest went off to college having been an independent learner for every single subject during high school. Math, chemistry, physics, literature, foreign language–she did them ALL completely by herself. All I did was grade her papers and chapter tests. (Which is true of everyone who has come after her, as well.) When it was time to do her first research paper in college, the idea of independent learning, i.e., taking the initiative, was so ingrained in her that she made an appointment with the college librarian to get a tour of the library and learn how to use its resources. This was not a requirement for any class–she just did it, as if it were a normal thing for a college freshman to do, because she knew she needed more skills in order to successfully complete the research paper assignment. Can you say "proud mama moment"?

This is the type of thing that independent learning fosters.

8) Which brings up the idea that independent learning prepares your child for college, because that is what college is. College students are expected to take responsibility for their own work, grades, completion of assignments, etc. No college professor is going to hold their hand or even notice if they are struggling, most likely. The student is expected to follow the syllabus, do the work, find outside resources, and ask for help when they need it. If they are used to it being this way at home, then they won't feel like they are in over their head in college.

This means that independent learning is one of the key things you can do in your high school homeschool to be more confident that you are indeed preparing your teen for college or life after homeschool. As you allow them to stretch their wings, to try, maybe fail, but to keep pressing on–all within the safety of your reach–you'll see them gain their own confidence, which is an important foundation to have before going out into the big world. And you'll feel better about how you're helping them to get ready.

How to Teach Independent Learning

How to teach this skill? What follows is a step-by-step approach. It is more focused on starting in the earlier years, though, because if you're reading this book and have younger kids, it will be very helpful. If your kid is in high school and still looking to you to teach them every subject, then read it anyway–and I'll jump in later with ideas for how to handle your specific situation.

1) You can start as soon as they can read independently. We started our eldest in about second grade, because that was when her younger sister started kindergarten and needed more of my time to learn to read. Not to mention the three even younger than that who DEFINITELY needed mom to help them through their day, LOL.

But beginning later is NOT a problem. Many moms like to keep the family together for many, if not most or all, subjects when the kids are in the elementary years. This is totally fine.

With an older child, the process of teaching them independent learning may actually go faster than if they were younger. On the other hand, the danger may be that since they are so used to having you teach them, they may balk at doing it themselves. And we know that middle schoolers and teens are pretty good at balking, LOL.

So when to start is up to you — use your best judgment regarding your child's needs and your goals for your family.

2) Begin with one subject only. This is a PROCESS, y'all. Don't tell your kid one day that they are on their own for everything, LOL. Baby steps.

How to choose which subject? Well, that depends a lot on which curriculum you are using. Some curriculums lend themselves well to independent learning; others really need mom to teach and facilitate.

We always started with math. We used ABeka math in the early years, because it was bright and colorful, and the workbooks were easy to write in. But if you are doing a math curriculum that relies heavily on manipulatives, then you might not want to choose math as the first subject for your child to learn independently.

(That is one positive aspect of workbooks and textbooks — it is much easier to foster independent learning with them. Unit studies, unschooling, Charlotte Mason, etc. do seem to require more hands-on time from mom, so you might have to adapt this process in creative ways to make it happen with those types of curriculum.)

Other possible subjects to start with would be English, handwriting, spelling — even science or history if the child is mostly reading and answering questions with those. Subjects for which the child is notebooking can also work well.

3) The actual process of teaching this skill happens in three steps: reading/watching the lesson, guided practice, and independent practice. It involves you gradually easing yourself out of their learning process over time. This is not something you have to plan on paper; just follow the flow and take cues from your child about when you can ease off and let them handle more and more on their own.

a) The first few days or weeks, have them read/watch the lesson alone and then ask them a few questions to see if they understood it. Once you feel fairly confident that they are comprehending without any prompting from you, you can stop asking them about it.

b) At the beginning, do help them answer the first few questions or problems. This is called "guided practice." It helps identify any areas they might not fully understand and gives you the chance to fill in any gaps. Work with them long enough, with them taking over more of the solving/answering process with each successive problem/question, until they can do one completely on their own while you "stand by."

This step should not happen for the entire lesson. Only help them through a FEW of the questions or problems. Even if they feel like they aren't ready to move onto the next step, you may have to push them a little bit. Remember, this is something they've never done before, so they may want to lean on you a bit. Be strong!

c) Then set them loose to do the rest of the problems or answers on their own. This is the "independent practice" part. But again, doing baby steps is key. So for awhile you will want them to check the answer WITH YOU after EVERY ONE. This prevents them doing the whole page while making the same mistake over and over again. You will catch it the first time, and the second time, LOL, so hopefully it won't happen a third time.

This routine — have them read on their own, test their comprehension, do guided practice of a few questions, then check each problem one at a time — can go on for as long or as little as you like. Use your kid as a guide — if they get comfortable quickly, then you don't need to spend much time in this phase. If they like having you there for each step, then stay there for awhile. But eventually you will want to kick them out of the nest, so to speak, and move onto the next phase.

4) Now it's time to turn them loose with the answer key and have them do ALL the problems on their own, checking THEMSELVES after each one. Again, checking after each one is CRUCIAL, at least for awhile, so they can make sure they don't waste a lot of time doing something all wrong and only finding out at the end. You wanna talk about frustration for everyone…

Just a quick note here: The answer key is an IMPORTANT learning tool. Do not consider it to be only mom's property, so that the kid may not consult it upon pain of death.

No, obviously we do not want our kids to cheat by looking at the key and writing down the answer without even doing the problem. But AFTER they have done the work, checking it right away is providing the feedback they need to foster learning.

And sometimes, when they are stuck on something and just can't get it, the answer key will give them the information they need to figure out what would have been the correct procedure. Then they can try the next problem using that procedure.

Here's another thing that is completely okay and should be encouraged: looking back at the text. Even in math, this can be a very profitable practice. Do you want them asking you EVERY question they have? Then YOU would not be enjoying the benefits of independent learning, LOL.

For many questions, the answer is found in a lesson they completed previously and may have forgotten a detail or two about. They should learn to try to find the answer themselves in the textbook and use you as a last resort. You can teach them how to use the table of contents and the index to find places to look. This is a GREAT skill for them to learn.

Eventually they may not need to check the answer key after EVERY problem or question. In math it may be a good idea anyway, depending on your child, but in other subjects they can probably complete the entire question set before checking their work. And so they will proceed day after day, completing the lessons in the curriculum all by their little selves. It's a great thing.

And then it becomes time to study for the chapter test, which is another facet of independent learning.

1) For math this is a simple matter of redoing several of the problems from each lesson, or completing a review set, if the book provides one. The child can pick and choose which problems to do, and how many of each, based on how confident they feel about each type of problem. The answer key (and solution manual, if provided) will be important resources in this process.

At first they may need your guidance to help them determine where they should focus. The goal is for the child to feel confident with each type of problem — and how to differentiate between the types of solutions required — before taking the test. I usually schedule one to two study days before the test to have time to reach this point.

Realize, too, that the test itself is a tool for learning. If they don't do well (and remember, we talked about this earlier: in our household, "not good" meant below an 80. Anything above that was fine), it is an opportunity to fall back and regroup, studying the areas of difficulty, and try again with a different test form. If they pass with no difficulty, that is feedback that they need to feel confident tackling the new topics of the next chapter. It's a win-win — even though it may be difficult for your child to see it that way sometimes, LOL.

2) In other subjects, there may be more instruction needed from you about best study practices. I always started this process in seventh grade. Before then I never expected the child to be able to read a text and study for a test. I think the elementary years should be much freer than that. But I have always felt that middle school is a great opportunity to gently prepare for high school.

I have found the Apologia science books, starting with Exploring Creation with General Science, to be great tools for teaching how to study for a test. They do provide a chapter review and study guide, but these don't give an indication of exactly what will be on the test, so the child still needs to study more in order to do well. The following process is what I use for Apologia, but you can adapt it over any subject and with any curriculum.

Initially, I don't expect them to do the first test on their own with no help and get an A. This would be an exercise in frustration. Instead I let them take the test completely open book. This gives them the flavor of taking a test, and they see how the test covers an entire chapter of material — but they don't need to stress about knowing everything.

For chapter two they have to memorize the vocabulary words. They can take the rest of the test open book, but first they need to write out those vocab definitions with the book closed.

For chapter three, I pick a section of the chapter that they have to study for mastery, and those questions on the test must be done without the book (in addition to the vocabulary words). I show them different study techniques, and they spend time implementing them for just that small quantity of material.

Then, over the course of the first semester, as they complete chapter after chapter, I make them responsible to study and know more and more. By the start of second semester they are taking the entire test without the book–but maybe for a test or two they get the option to pull out the book for anything they don't remember. They have to mark the question(s) on the test they did that for.

Do you see how it's a process? By the end of 7th grade year, if not before, the child is studying for and taking a difficult science test with NO help from me. So now for the subject of science over the rest of their home-school education, they will be learning independently. Including Chemistry, y'all. High school science? DONE.

Starting Independent Learning in High School

So, if you've read that all through like I suggested, and you have younger children, you are now all set to prepare them for high school way before they get there. But if your kid is IN high school and independent learning has not been a thing for either of you yet, you are probably freaking out a little by now.

NO WORRIES. We are striving to stay sane and even enjoy these years, and so we can work with your situation just the way it is. Hang in there–deep breaths–and let's talk about this.

The first thing to note is that curriculum choice has a lot to do with whether independent learning happens or not. Some curricula is very dependent on teacher preparation or actual hands-on time from mom during the lesson. Other choices do the prep and instruction for you. Textbooks, video curriculum, online classes, community college classes–all of these mean you can be out of the picture much more easily. I have several to recommend on the resource page for this book found on my blog.

NO, you do not need to sit with your kid every day and learn alongside them so that you will be knowledgeable and can help when they have a question. A first step towards independent learning is to tell them to look back in the chapter or review the video again to see if they can find a clue to help get over their hump. Maybe you'll need to help them do that the first few times, because your average teen may very well balk at this if they haven't been used to it–usually accompanied by some sort of whine or wail, LOL.

Often, they have just overlooked some small detail which you can uncover by doing a quick scan of the chapter. I don't know why it is, but they will claim to have looked a gazillion times, but you as the adult will often find it almost immediately. After awhile they will, too. It's a skill, I think, and we've just practiced it more. Or we don't have emotion/frustration clouding our vision. However, as a side note, realize that this process will take a lot of patience on your part, so decide to stock up on it right now. Just sayin'.

Also be aware that if you've been hand-holding your teen and have never really given them the chance to try learning on their own, then they can probably handle more than you think they can. It's worth a try to let them see what they can do on their own. I think you'll be pleasantly surprised by how much you can almost immediately hand over to them.

With a teen, you can do the same steps that I outlined above for younger kids–which is why I had you read that section, so if you skipped it, go back and read it now–but just speed up the process A LOT. For instance, it may take your teen only one or two days to understand how to read the lesson and do the problems by themselves. The first day could be reading, guided practice, and independent practice, and then if that goes super easily, the second day you could maybe skip the guided practice altogether.

I would caution against turning the whole thing over to them the first day–the sink or swim approach–which might be tempting. I think it is wise to check their work for the first few days before you let them do that on their own. But if you want to have them read/watch and try to do the problems/ questions without you, as a diagnostic process of whether they're ready or not and where the difficulties lie, then I think that's reasonable. Every kid is different, and you are the best judge of what your teen can handle.

Don't try to jump into independent learning with more than one subject at a time, though, and do start with a subject that they already have a high level of confidence in. I know this is probably obvious, but I think it's worth stating anyway. If your teen is not used to doing this by now, their level of confidence about it may be quite low. Don't overwhelm them. Remind them that you are in this together, and you won't turn them loose until you think they're ready–which may not be the same thing as when THEY think they're ready, LOL. But that's okay–sometimes you gotta be the strong one and let them try, stumble, and possibly fall... and then figure out how to pick themselves back up again. These life lessons are just as valuable as the academic content they are trying to learn.

Or their level of confidence might be very high–"yo Mom, I've got this"– but I would caution against taking their word for it right away, LOL. Again, I think it's important to check their work for a little while, until they are proving to you that they are in fact learning what they need to and aren't just "checking the box." Don't expect perfection, but do look for enough of a competence level that they can correct their mistakes fairly quickly and then move onto the next lesson without missing foundational concepts/ information.

When they've shown you that they can understand the material well enough to do the assignment for the lesson reasonably successfully, then they are probably able to take over the task of grading their own daily work. Just be sure that correcting mistakes–or at the very least understanding why they occurred–is a non-negotiable part of completing the lesson.

When you've reached this stage with one subject, then add another. Or maybe, if they've taken to the process like a duck to water, you can add more than one subject. Again, take a few days to correct their daily work yourself before you set them loose to be completely on their own.

Probably within the course of a semester or less, you'll have your average teen functioning at a high capacity completely independently. I'm not guaranteeing A-level work, because this has nothing to do with academic ability. I am saying that they will be handling their own learning, with you as merely their supervisor and question-answerer rather than their teacher or fellow student or hand-holder. And this is a really wonderful place to be!

Your Part of the Process

One caution, though: The homeschool parent does need to exercise due diligence by checking in with their teen on a regular basis. Don't just set them loose and walk away, not to return until weeks or months later. It is necessary, especially as you are starting this process, to be their accountability person, to make sure they are reporting to you what they're doing and that you are seeing actual work occurring.

Don't just take their word for it; ask to see their notebook. Look over their math lesson and make a point of counting to make sure all the problems are there, with no question marks. See if they've made notes on the science video. Do they have an outline done for their paper? Go back to the math again and make sure they actually have things marked WRONG, LOL. Checking their daily work is just as important as doing it, hello.

There is a fine line here between being a nag and supervising, and it's okay if you sometimes seem to err on the nagging side. As you see your teen being diligent, you can back off some. If you see them falling behind, though, then you can catch it before it becomes a larger problem.

Also–and this is very important–keep up with grading the things they give to you to grade. Get that math test or history paper back to them within a day or two. Set an example for consistency. Don't be a "do as I say not as I do" in this one thing, okay?

Yes, with independent learning you can have the easiest years of your homeschool career, but that doesn't mean you can get off scot-free with nothing to do at all. Your teen still needs you, even if they won't admit it. Be the parent and stick with them.

Another way to do this is just to sit in the same room where they are working, doing your own thing, so that they know you are available if they have questions. Whatever it takes so that they know without a doubt that you are keeping an eye on them and want them to succeed.

Otherwise, you might find yourself in one of the following scenarios (names have been withheld to protect the guilty):

1) You might get behind with the grading. Not hard to fix, but a pain nonetheless.

2) (Corollary 1) You finally get to the grading after a lapse of several weeks and discover that your teen has no clue what they are doing. This is NOT fun.

3) (Corollary 2) Your kid might claim to be doing all their work, and then you find out weeks later (due to not keeping up yourself) that they in fact were not. This is SUPER not fun.

Trust me when I tell you that you don't want to find yourself in any of these situations. So yes, independent learning has some absolutely wonderful benefits, and I believe it is truly the best way to homeschool through high school. But it does also have some potential pitfalls. Just stay on top of your (now much smaller!) portion of the work, and you'll all be much happier. Take it from someone who has learned the hard way. Um.

Curriculum Considerations

One thing you may be wondering about is what to use for curriculum when you want your teen to learn more independently. And I'm here to say that what you've heard about acceptable/not acceptable ways to homeschool high school isn't necessarily true.

In the homeschool world there is a lot of talk about "it's homeschool, not school at home." And I get that; I really do. When possible, it is really neat to be able to dive into what we want to study in this freeform, discovery style that everyone seems to tout as the perfect way to homeschool.

But ya know what? I personally have no problem with "school at home."

I think textbooks have been given a bad rap. I personally used LOTSA textbooks in our homeschool, especially in high school. The fact that I was the one who chose them, and my kids didn't have to learn what the public school officials said they should, was enough of a positive for me that I wasn't too concerned about whether we were "discovering" or "making learning fun" or being "delight-directed" or whatever else is acclaimed out there.

And frankly, as already alluded to, I was generally looking to reduce my workload. To me, just showing the kids a bookshelf (or the INTERNET, hello) and saying "have at it" was going to cause MORE work for mom, not less. I was overwhelmed just thinking about it.

I realize I'm being a little bit simplistic here. And the truth is, if I had the earlier years to do over again, I would probably have made them more "fun," but the high school years? Not so much.

Textbooks lend themselves to independent learning so much more easily than any other form of curriculum other than an online class or video course. The structure is already there; all you have to do is plan out what will happen when. Or have your teen do that, if they are capable of it. In the effort to make high school more doable for everyone and to encourage your teen to take ownership of their own education, I see textbooks as a great help.

Textbooks are used in college, after all. There is no reason not to start using them in high school, aside from the often impossibly-high ideals placed in front of us by all the Pinterest-perfect homeschoolers out there. Don't feel guilty or "less than" if you want to structure your teen's learning by having them use a textbook for a given course–or even for all of their courses, if that's what is working best for you.

The point of this chapter (the whole book, really) is to encourage you that homeschooling high school can be easier than you have been imagining. When your teen is doing most of the work on their own, there is much less reason to be stressed. YOU are not responsible for your teen's education; they are. You are just the mentor and the recorder of grades. This idea takes a huge load off, doesn't it?

Jill:

My son did 100% independent learning in high school except for two co-op classes for literature. I consider myself a manager by the teen years. I write out the weekly plan and they decide when and how the work will be done and I verify their work by putting my own eyes on it. What I did not check, however, was often ignored. All three of my girls are fantastic independent learners.

Angie:

My son gained more independence as he progressed through high school. In ninth grade, he was still reliant on me to push him to do assignments and to give instruction. By his senior year, he only needed occasional help—usually in the form of helping drill for a test or teaching about research paper formats. By then, he was getting most of his instruction from outside sources—college classes and co-op—or independent study.

Enrolling in a good co-op pushed my son out of the "14-year-old boy slump" and exposed him to teachers who excelled in areas I don't. This was not an easy transition. He would have preferred to stay home. But he graduated with a clear direction for his future and more confidence in his abilities. He credits that co-op and a few teacher-moms and dads who invested their time and expertise in their students.

7 // SOCIALIZATION FOR TEENS

There it is again–the S word. But it's not the four-letter one that we teach our kids not to say while secretly whispering it to ourselves in moments of stress. It's the longer one that has been a homeschool hot button for decades. Let's say it all together now: SOCIALIZATION.

One person corrected me about this recently. She said "socialization" is "the process of learning to behave in a way that is acceptable to society." So, she claimed, instead of talking about providing "socialization activities" for our kids, we should really be referring to them as "social" activities.

She might have a valid point. But here's mine in return: everyone uses the word "socialization" as the buzzword when it comes to homeschooling. Nobody is concerned about whether homeschoolers are being social; rather, they contend about whether homeschoolers are being socialized. To me, it doesn't matter if anyone is using the terms correctly or not. I think we need to realize that the outside world needs to be educated about BOTH.

The concern seems to be that kids won't be socialized OR social if they are schooled at home. They won't be socialized–i.e., learn how to work and play well with others–because they won't have sufficient social opportunities to practice (because they are "stuck" at home all day). Either or both, really, is the issue–so I don't think we need to get too nitpicky about the term we're using. The world outside of homeschooling just doesn't understand either way, and we often buy into what they're saying because we aren't used to thinking about things any differently. My job here is to dispel the myths and give us practical ideas to work with. So let's do that.

We all know—or if we don't, then let me help, LOL—that discussing whether homeschooled elementary or middle school kids are "socialized" is actually pretty silly. Kids at that age who are homeschooled are no less able to converse or interact than kids from brick-and-mortar schools. In fact, they usually have more opportunities to be social with people of all different stages of life, because they aren't mandatorily segregated into age groups. They also aren't influenced negatively by being forced to spend large amounts of time with kids who have difficulty with self-control or who are just plain not nice.

Yet even though we understand that about our younger kids, we often think it doesn't apply to high school. We believe our teens need more socialness (there, is that a decent compromise? LOL) than they used to when they were smaller. We are concerned that they won't get the social/socialization opportunities that we had—the activities specific to the teen years that we think they need in order to become well-rounded individuals.

There is some validity to that perspective. I personally think teens do have a larger need (or maybe just a desire, but it's a strong one) for relationships and interaction—and especially with other teens. They want friendships. They want to get out of the house. They like activity. They get bored easily. They crave discussions with other teens about movies, music, clothes, electronics, airsoft, whatever. Their younger siblings just don't cut it for this purpose anymore. And the parents are downright embarrassing, LOL. They (WE) don't know much these days, am I right?

So what do we do about this? The good news is that this is a very fixable issue, one that we don't need to be overwhelmed about. If homeschooling high school is important to us—if our WHY is compelling enough—then we can find a way to meet our teen's desire for interaction with other teens. And in the process we'll feel better about their growth as an individual, as well.

One thing that may be true is that mom may need to put forth some effort to make this happen. If the teen does not have enough naturally-occurring interaction with other teens, then mom may need to take some initiative. Look around in your area for clubs, sports, volunteering opportunities, places to work, etc. that your teen might be interested in. Maybe facilitate something yourself, if you see a gap and are willing to fill it. Reach out to other moms of teens. Organize a group for skating or to go to a movie. Offer to drive your teen where they want to go, if they are unable to do it themselves.

But don't feel guilty if you can't do everything. If facilitating is NOT your cup of tea, don't feel like you have to. There is enough out there to find for your teen to do that doesn't run you ragged or take you too far outside your comfort zone. I live very rurally, and I'm a fairly lazy person–and if I can give my kids social opportunities, then so can just about anyone.

Sometimes we do have to evaluate if our comfort zone needs adjusting; for instance, I have to be willing to drive an hour each way to co-op once a week, when I would of course rather drive much less. But other times we can legitimately say no and look for something that fits the needs of ALL of us better. We talked in Chapter 1 about how to evaluate if something fits your family, so I won't belabor it again here.

I asked the members of my Facebook group to list what their kids do for socialization/social activities. Surely there is something on this list that would fit your kid, something that you can handle making it possible for them. Take a look:

1. tech club, IT club, robotics, STEM challenges club
2. local library events — gaming, teen advisory board
3. team sports — all kinds!! Football, softball, soccer, baseball, basketball, lacrosse, etc. — even curling, roller derby, and water polo were mentioned. There are local homeschool teams, travel teams, or recreational leagues; in some states they can participate at the public school. Sports are basically everywhere in some way, shape, or form.
4. individual sports — gymnastics, track, cross country, swimming, bowling, archery, fencing, surfing, power skating, tennis
5. getting a job, whether only during the summer or part-time year-round
6. church activities — youth group, worship choir/band, drama team, Awana, handbells, Royal Rangers, youth retreats, Bible quiz team, missions trip, Young Life, lunch after service (LOL)
7. summer camp — whether as an attendee or a counselor
8. Boy Scouts, Girl Scouts, Venture scouts (co-ed)

9. roller skating, ice skating
10. 4H, also dairy and livestock judging
11. classes at the local craft store — art, cake decorating, sewing, knitting, crochet
12. homeschool co-op classes and activities
13. martial arts of all kinds
14. dance — swing dance, ballet, jazz, tap, ballroom
15. clubs built around a school subject — history, science, geography, math
16. community theater — acting, stagehand, sound, lights
17. clubs built around an interest — chess, books, writing, board games, Dungeons & Dragons, rock climbing, ukulele, Rubik's cube, welding
18. activities built around shooting — airsoft wars, nerf battles, paintball, laser tag, gun range
19. dual enrollment
20. yard or field games — kick the can, flag football, ghost in the graveyard, frisbee football, capture the flag
21. recreational swimming at community pool or beach
22. mini golf
23. hosting a foreign exchange student or Fresh Air Fund kid
24. fall fest, hayride
25. group texting, Skype, Google hangouts
26. teen events at homeschool conference
27. political activism
28. dog training (including service dogs), dog showing
29. bingo
30. working the family business
31. X-box live, online video games
32. homeschool prom
33. leadership programs — Toastmasters, Teen Pact, Kiwanis Key Club, Beta Club, Patriot Academy, Trail Life USA,
34. 5K runs
35. study groups
36. mock trial, speech and debate
37. community education classes — Spanish, photography, sign language
38. field trips

39. park days
40. Science Olympiad
41. escape room
42. bonfire
43. going to a movie
44. meeting for ice cream or coffee
45. yard work party
46. car wash
47. u-pick apples, berries
48. going to a museum, aquarium, historical site
49. star gazing, comet watching
50. hanging out at the mall, shopping
51. science labs for school
52. classes at the zoo
53. Civil War reenacting
54. boating clubs — rowing, sailing
55. group travel
56. participating in parades
57. carpooling
58. horseback riding lessons, equestrian team
59. gym membership, exercise classes, yoga
60. career night
61. National League of Junior Cotillions
62. going to a video game arcade
63. making and selling a product
64. "extreme" sports — indoor skydiving, parkour
65. hosting a food-based activity — ice cream social, potluck dinner, chili cook-off, tea party, progressive dinner, mystery dinner, make-your-own pizza, Christmas cookie baking/exchange, picnic
66. jumping at the local trampoline center
67. ziplining
68. fishing
69. biking, mountain biking
70. vegetable gardening
71. geocaching
72. scavenger hunt
73. hiking, wild edible foraging (just be sure they know what they're look-

ing for! Yikes!)
74. river stomping — I'm not sure what this is, but it sounds fun, LOL.
75. sleepovers
76. music lessons — piano, violin, guitar, voice, drums, basically any instrument you can think of
77. community youth music groups — orchestra, band, choir
78. making videos
79. American Heritage Girls
80. YMCA — classes, sports, whatever else
81. Department of Conservation youth activities, nature/environmental program at local farm
82. teen military clubs — Sea Cadets, Civil Air Patrol
83. Police Explorers, Fire Explorers
84. being a penpal
85. volunteer work — library, humane shelter, soup kitchen, food bank, senior center, crisis pregnancy center, Sunday School/VBS, Ronald McDonald House, wildlife refuge, petting zoo, babysitting for women's event, post office, fire station, community service projects
86. camps based on a particular interest — space camp, art camp, music camp, sports camp
87. inviting another family over for board games, card games, lunch, dinner, a movie — whatever!
88. acting lessons
89. babysitting, pet sitting
90. community youth Bible study
91. cheerleading
92. meet to run, walk, or do an exercise video
93. online classes
94. attending a concert, sports event, musical, rodeo
95. having a party — costume, birthday, halloween, Christmas, graduation, end-of-school-year
96. crafting get-together — stamping, Christmas ornaments
97. trick-or-treating, Christmas caroling, Easter egg hunt
98. phone texting, social media
99. snowboarding, skiing, sledding,snowball fights
100. just hanging out! Not to be overlooked, LOL.

Notice that a lot of these are activities that mom can facilitate. Having some kind of gathering at the house or forming a club based around an interest are both relatively easy things to put together. Finding teens to do this with may be the tough part, but it's not insurmountable. What about posting a notice at the library, or reaching out to a family at church that you don't know very well?

For the introvert mom, this can be more difficult to feel comfortable with, and that's okay. But if your concern is for your kid NOT to share your same worries/fears/awkwardness in social situations, then maybe it's worth the effort to step out of your comfort zone. That's up to you to decide.

Here's one thing that we all need to remember: it's not just homeschooled teens who may struggle socially. In fact, many homeschooled teens don't struggle at all. Just like in the public/private schools, some teens are socially awkward and some are not. We all remember the cliques of the popular kids and then the outlier kids who had difficulty fitting in. Which were you?

If you felt like high school was one of the worst experiences of your life, or if you envied the girls who always looked good and/or got all the boys' attention or just always seemed to have great friendships–why should your kid be any different? Maybe they would still be like that in the brick-and-mortar school setting. I firmly believe that there is most likely the same proportion of introverts in the homeschool world as there is in the public school world. Let's not blame homeschooling for something that may just be genetics.

I had to remind my 15-year-old of that the other day. "Sorry, kiddo, but the apple doesn't fall that far from the tree. I was weird in high school. I did not fit in or feel comfortable. It's not surprising that you feel that way, too. Some of that might be attributable to homeschooling, but it's very possible that it is just the way you are, because you are my daughter. Them's the breaks, and I wish I could help. But I can definitely empathize, if that means anything."

Or perhaps it's those of us who struggled socially in public school that are more prone to homeschool through high school anyway. I know that was a big reason for my husband and I. My memories of high school are full of anxiety, frustration, sadness, loneliness, etc. etc.–why would I want that for my kids? Again, we can't blame the homeschooling alone if our kids turn out to have the same issues with this that we did.

One thing that has proven true for all of my kids who have graduated–they did find their niche after high school. Those who went to college found their besties there, those who went to work found friends there. Being homeschooled did not cripple them socially for life.

In fact, my personal opinion is that homeschooling through high school gave their personalities a more solid foundation, so that they were more comfortable in their own skin before they had to brave the scary, wide world. During the teen years, the hormonally-charged angst is real, and the desire to fit in is strong. Peer pressure is definitely a thing. I didn't want to expose my kids to it until they were more able to stand strong in their own individuality, which I think the added years of being home gave them.

When you think about it, the alternatives to homeschooling don't actually provide TRUE socialization. Instead, teens are locked into peer groups of similar age and academic ability, and they are exposed not only to acceptable ways to behave but also to many of the inacceptable ones. Drugs, bullying, teen sex, cliques, grouping into jocks vs. cheerleaders vs. geeks vs. goths–I don't even know what they're all called these days.

In my time, we had a contingent we called the "greasers," who wore "greaser-boots" (which were actually just hiking boots, hello) and flannel shirts and who smoked behind the school. We had the jocks and the cheerleaders–they were the popular ones that we all looked up to; and we had the "preps" who were our fashion leaders (because the preppy look was in–I really wanted pants with whales on them like one of the other girls had!). I won't even mention what we called the kids who were involved in music or theater, of which I was one. Kids still do this stereotyping today. How is this considered positive "socialization"? I have to say that I am not a fan.

As parents, it's important to remember that we are aware of the big picture, while our teens often are not. We know that things will change after high school. We know that these years seem long but will actually pass quite quickly. We know that our kids are interesting people who have lots going for them.

Which brings up another point: Are you praising your kid and building them up? We'll discuss this more in the next chapter, but I think it fits here, too.

One of the reasons teens crave being social is that they need the affirmation that comes from being accepted by other people. They want to be complimented on their clothes or their athletic ability or their grades. They want to know what makes them special. They like the feeling of making someone laugh. They are looking for ways to feel better about themselves, and they think social-ness will give that to them.

We as parents can and should provide affirmation, even though, as mine have said, "You're my MOM. That doesn't count." YES, IT DOES. I mean, I do understand that in their little brains, they feel like it would be more valuable coming from someone else, but I'm quite certain that they still do register those encouraging words from us somewhere in their heart-of-hearts. Give them what they're searching for. Let them know that you think they're pretty great.

Not just "I love you,"–although of course, say that often–but also "Hey, lookin' good today!" Or "Wow, what a great tackle that was!" and "This paragraph rocks!" and "Mmmmm, these cookies are yummy!" Be specific. Compliment their hair or their clothes or their driving or their smile–basically, just try to pile on the praise whenever you can. Don't make things up, LOL, but don't always be the mom who wants her kid to improve. Be the friend who tells them you like who they are RIGHT NOW.

Part of that is to follow your teen's lead about the whole social thing. If your teen prefers to stay at home, it's not that necessary to force them to get out. There will come a time soon enough when you'll wish they spent any time at home. Of course, I'm not talking about if they go into a deep funk or depression or there is a legitimate concern about their emotional well-being; obviously in that case, you need to pull the parent card and get them the help you think they need. But for the teen who just isn't interested in meeting tons of new people all the time or in putting themselves forward, it's okay to continue laying low for awhile. Be glad that they're satisfied with family life and trust that they will bloom socially when they are ready.

On the other hand, if your teen is constantly complaining of being bored or that they never get out of the house, then certainly try to honor their requests in this area. Do what you can to help. Don't hold them back if they're ready for a taste of the larger world. Giving them more freedom socially can help keep the gears of homeschooling running more smoothly.

On Transportation & Telephones

One way to facilitate your teen being social is to not balk at them getting their driver's license. I know this might seem like it's coming from left field, but it really does have an impact here. Sometimes those apron strings can be tied pretty tight, can't they? And driving is scary, because so much can go wrong, and sometimes does. As a mom this is one of the hardest things–to watch your inexperienced teen drive down the road away from you for the first time, or even the hundredth time! But we all have to do it sooner or later.

I'm not saying to allow it before your child is ready, and only you can be the judge of that. And I can't promise they will come to no harm; I wish I could, but I can't. All I can say is that allowing them to drive is a healthy stage of personal development for both them and you. Being able to drive empowers teens to make the social stuff happen for themselves, leaving you free to do whatever else you prefer to do. They don't feel as dependent on you, and they can be super creative when you have given them rein to be.

One way to spark their creativity and get them involved socially is to put the planning on THEM. Nowadays, if my kids want to do something, I tell them to have at it. I'll be around if they have questions or need advice, and to help choose a good time to schedule the activity, but the rest is up to them. They have to plan out the schedule, provide the food, clean the house—everything. I'll be present to be the chaperone, but they need to be the ones in charge.

This has resulted in really epic all-day airsoft events at our house, when everyone who attended said they had a blast. Also game nights, sleepovers, etc.–and I barely had to lift a finger for any of it. That's my kind of socialization, LOL.

Having a phone can be another valid way for a teen to be social. I know that this can also be a temptation to idleness and improper communication, but first let's talk about the positives.

I personally am unable to let my teens drive out of the driveway without knowing they have some way to communicate with me if they have any kind of trouble, whether it be a problem with the car, or an accident, or somebody creepy in the store, or whether to buy the blue sweater or the red one. Any and all of the above is something that I want them to be able to talk to me about right away if they feel the need or want to. A cellphone provides that safety net which I did not have when I was their age.

One of my vivid memories from my tween years was when I got dropped off at the mall with a friend of mine, who was spotted shoplifting as we browsed through a store. I had no idea such a thing could happen or that one of my friends would actually do it. I was shocked and quite freaked out. As an innocent party, it was not necessary for me to stay in the back room of the store where they had detained her; they were calling the cops and she was going to be taken by police car to the local station. I had to call someone to pick me up–which in the midst of my emotional distress involved digging out the nine pennies I had left, asking the mean detective lady for one more, finding a payphone outside the store, and calling home, all the while desperately hoping that someone would be there to pick up. I don't want any of my kids to go through something like that without the certain knowledge that they can use their cellphone (without worrying about finding money), and that I will be at the other end of their call, no matter where I am.

In our family, the first child did not receive her own cellphone until she was learning to drive. And it wasn't a smart phone–did they even exist back then? I don't remember, LOL. But regardless, it was just a basic phone that she lived with for a few years. Following her, the next two children each got their own phone as they in turn learned to drive–it was the one from the sibling above, handed down–unless they wanted to pay out of their own money for something better. As often happens in parenting, the procedure ended up being different for the later children: One got his phone when he started a job, even though he wasn't driving yet; and the last got hers at an even younger age, because by this time we had no landline, and she was being left alone at the house sometimes.

Another reason our youngest was given a phone at an earlier age was that phones are more of a thing now than they were even 8+ years ago, when my oldest turned 16. You just can't deny that cellphones are part of the social life of a teen these days. Texting alone is huge, and don't forget all the social media apps and the music and YouTube and games... so yeah.

All of that, of course, brings out the issue of the kid being on the phone TOO MUCH. And I completely get that. I think as a parenting generation this whole cellphone thing has come upon us unawares. I personally had no idea that it would be such a hard thing to deal with. I didn't see it coming, so I didn't plan ahead. I was not proactive, and so now there is more work to do than if I had prevented overuse from becoming a thing in the first place. Anyone with me?

I feel like we're caught between a rock and a hard place. I know we lived without cellphones ourselves, so theoretically it should not be a prob- lem for our kids to do so, too. But we had an abundance of payphones around; and also it was not as scary a proposition to flag down a stranger when you were broken down on the side of the road, or to walk up to an unknown house and ask to use the phone. These days no one wants their kid to do that. Yikes!

So although taking away the phone is supposed to be a wonderful disciplinary tactic, I've never done it. I suppose you could take it away while they're at home and then give it back whenever they go out, but to me that seems complicated and therefore unworkable. Especially because, since I work outside the home, they are often at home without me, and I need to be able to communicate with them.

I'm sure there are parents out there who are reading this right now who have this whole thing under control and can't understand why it's even an issue. All I can say to that is that they might want to just skip this part of the chapter, then. I think for many of us it's not a simple thing to figure out. As we like to say in our house, imitating Mike Wazowski from Monsters, Inc., "It's a work in progress."

I do think when you take a cellphone away from a teen, you are taking away one of their big avenues for being social. And I don't think that should be taken lightly or done at the drop of a hat. There is a fine line to be navigated here, between being the parent who "knows what is best"–are we ALWAYS right?–and being sensitive to their legitimate desire for interaction in the outside world.

My Facebook group is a huge resource for advice for things like this (I've consulted them a lot about this chapter, LOL, because there is such a wide range of possibilities about this topic). I asked them for their solutions for conquering the "my teen spends too much time on the cellphone" beast. Here is a sampling of the responses from there:

We've tried to make it their goal. Screens are junk food, like potato chips. Your body cannot operate well on a steady diet. Your mind does not do well on a steady diet of junk food either. You need to balance it. Be aware of how much time you spend eating junk food.

We have rules about the phone, but truthfully, nothing works but me monitoring and limiting usage. I'm hoping that as maturity comes, so will self-discipline and restraint.

The phone is not allowed to be used until school and chores are done. It is to be put away at a designated time at night. No devices at meal time. We use Covenant Eyes to monitor usage, and we periodically make checks of the phone. Honestly, we're too busy for there to be overuse of the phone. My daughter loves to read so she prefers a book over a video game. No social media yet–joint decision–she's not interested in it since she sees it as a waste of time. She does Hangouts with her friends instead.

Cellphones are not allowed upstairs at night, they get charged in the kitchen. I have access to all social media & email accounts and privileges are lost if you change a password and don't notify me of the change. I spot check messages and friends/follow lists. Inappropriate conversations will result in lost privileges, blocked contacts, or both.

I don't stress about it.

We have strict, simple rules for our kids. Things that are easy to monitor. NO phones upstairs. NO apps downloaded without permission. The kids don't have social media. NO texting people without getting permission to add that person to the 'ok to text' list. NO using phones in the car without permission. At night, we have a charging station downstairs for all phones. My kids are all involved in sports pretty heavily so it definitely helps that they don't have tons of time! My 15,12, and 10-year-old have phones. My 9-year-old does not.

My three kids share a phone. There are no games in it and the only apps are Google maps and Waze. They all use it to text their friends and they know that their siblings can see their texts because the phone isn't private.

We do no cellphones until schoolwork and chores are done and then they must turn them in to our bedroom by 9 pm.

Conversation has worked here and physically taking them away when that doesn't work. Hobbies work as well. My daughter has seen how her friends have become zombies she no longer wants to associate due to their phones, so that helped. We also have a "no electronics in your bedroom" policy.

I included a wide variety of responses, so that you can see that in this as in almost everything else we've talked about in this book, there is no one right way to deal with the cellphone issue. As always, do what works for you and your family.

Family Life

I do want to make at least one more point before we leave this chapter. I don't want anyone to come away from this discussion thinking that I have given up on family life altogether when it comes to teens. That is far, far away from what I intend. Just because our teen wants to get out into the wide, wide world doesn't mean we have to kill ourselves to make that happen. There is absolutely nothing wrong with expecting them to be content spending time with siblings and parents rather than running around town or closeting themselves in their room for hours a day.

I often find validation for what I am doing in life by comparing our current situation to that of the pioneers. LOL. To me, if it worked for the pioneers, then there is no reason for me to think that I have to do anything different. In the case of socialization, the pioneer teens didn't have much outside of family, did they? There were barn-raisings and the circuit rider coming in once a month and harvesting, and probably weddings and funerals–lotsa funerals, yikes–but it wasn't an everyday thing for them. They had their family, for the most part, and that was it. Yet they were actually considered capable of adult responsibilities and interaction without having to do a lot of practicing first, hello.

Yes, life is much more complicated now. But I think the principle still holds true: Our teens will figure out social interaction when it's necessary, without us needing to force it too much or rearrange our entire lives to facilitate it. They won't be warped for life. It's kinda like potty-training, LOL. Sometimes it takes a while–Ack! Just thinking about it gives me PTSD–but everyone figures it out sooner or later.

If they do get involved in something that is regularly scheduled, remember that it can very probably be used for high school credit. I'm not going to go into detail about that here, because I've already dealt with it thoroughly in *Cure the Fear*. Just remember that all that time they are spending can most likely be counted up and applied to their transcript in some way or another. So that might make all that driving more valuable to you, LOL!

The Best Way to Provide Socialization

If you're wondering which socialization/social activity would give you the most bang for your buck, I would have to say that having my teens get a part-time job has been the bestest thing ever. I rate it above music lessons (because though the teen is supposed to learn discipline to practice and cure the performance jitters, that didn't always work out for us, LOL), and I also rate having a job above just about everything else that I am familiar with on that huge list I gave you earlier.

Like most things in my parenting journey, we didn't learn the wonderful results that having a job can work in a teen until our last two kids (out of five). Sadly, it is a truth of my life that I did a much better job in just about every aspect of parenting with my last kid–from the very beginning of having my first great hospital stay after delivery, to not having as many fights about what clothes to put on during toddlerdom (because I was less concerned about looking like a mom who has it all together), to keeping my voice down (translated: not screaming) when I was angry, etc. I literally told her last night that I am a way better mom with her than I was with the others (implication: "So there!"), and she said, somewhat sarcastically, "Thanks, Mom. I do appreciate that." And we moved on...

We didn't let our oldest kids get "real" jobs outside the home as teens. We expected them to come up with some way to earn money that would further their career path or their abiding interest. No fast food joints or lifeguarding for them! And we knew best, doggone it. So the oldest, the violin player, began busking in the streets of downtown Branson. (For those who are unfamiliar with the word, busking is when a musician will perform on the street with their case open to receive tips.) When she did it, she did well, but it was nerve-wracking for her. It may have taught her initiative, I get that, but it was also very much a "throw you in the pond and see if you can swim" scenario–frightening, and not always easy to figure out how to tread water. Ya know?

The second child, our first athlete, technically worked for someone else, but it wasn't a traditional job where you get training and work up to things gradually. It was another sink-or-swim situation; she began reffing at the local recreational league pee-wee soccer games. Thankfully, there wasn't much to this, but for an introverted girl, it was freakingly scary. She held a post of authority against parents who (even with kids that young) could be intimidating about whether that ball was truly out or why their kid didn't get to throw it in. Again, it was decent money, and of course it taught her a little bit about dealing with people–but from her perspective, a fast-food joint would have been more tolerable.

The third child, freaked out by seeing what her sisters had to go through, never got a job at all. The standard of "it must relate to your career or main interest" was still in place, and for her to fulfill that, her options were limited. It was easier to just forget about the whole thing.

So along came number four, the only boy. When he turned 16, I knew we needed to do something different. The hubby and I had a talk, and it was agreed to let him apply to our local Chick-Fil-A. And the difference this made in our son's life was incredible.

First, he had regular money coming in. TEENS LOVE THIS. Our older girls had to carefully plan all of their purchases and never had enough to go around. The son was rolling in it. He became generous with trips to get ice cream and coffee, Christmas gifts were thoughtful and of high qual-ity, and he was able to finance his interests and grow them by purchasing better equipment. This was the same end result as we had been going for with our old rule, just a different way of getting there. Interesting, isn't it?

Second, he was taught a work ethic. He learned how to get himself to work on time–even early–every shift. He learned to show up and perform even when he was tired. He learned how to do a task thoroughly and well, even the nasty ones like cleaning pee or throw up in the tunnel of the play place. Yuck.

Third, and here we get to the social aspect–we discovered an extrovert in the family! My son was a bit scared at first about talking with people as part of the job, but it came only as he was prepared for it (not necessarily ready, but prepared, which can be two different things, if you know what I mean). Also, he had supervisors to help with any question that came up, so it wasn't as much of a do-or-die experience. And he grew to actually enjoy all the interaction. And as a result, we watched him grow from a sheltered homebody into a social young man.

Fourth, he made friends. In two weeks he will be a groomsman in the wedding of one of them. They have formed a D&D group, they go out for eats, he met one of them regularly for Bible study for awhile, etc.

So interestingly enough, when his younger sister was still 15 years old, we let her apply there, too. There was no more mention of "it should be about your career or interest" because we had seen the value to her brother. And now we are watching her grow by leaps and bounds, too. I wish we had figured this out earlier. That's one of my reasons for writing this book–so you can learn from my mistakes and don't have to make them yourself, LOL.

Obviously it's a good idea to choose very carefully the environment in which you want your kid to work. We didn't let them apply just anywhere. But I do think in hindsight that teens and part-time jobs are a good mix, and in my opinion they are the best way to provide socialization AND social activities for your teen. A job meets pretty much all of the goals you are hoping for, with the added benefit of that sense of accomplishment when the paycheck arrives, as well as possible credit for school. And you don't have to pay for everything anymore, LOL!

The socialization issue can be ongoing. It may take some time to find something that fits. I think it's worth the effort to keep looking until you find it, but if you don't, your teen will not be stunted or deprived. Don't feel guilty or stressed about it. The theme of this book is the idea that whatever you can do is great, but if you don't want to or can't, then let it go–and that applies to your teen's social life, as well. Truly!

JIll:

If socialization just means them visiting with people outside of our home then I'd say we do a lot. If it means peer groupings in sports or music then we did none.

Our children regularly interact with abundant family members of all ages-from foster babies to great grandparents and their cousins. They are at church serving children or making coffee weekly as well as attending youth events. We do not do sports or music and only did a small handful of co-op classes.

I may do more with my younger children when they are teens because I won't be so busy with younger children who needed more time at home.

Angie:

Homeschooled kids and public schooled kids struggle with social interaction, some more than others. Sometimes family issues or health will affect a teen's willingness and ability to socialize. Our family went through some serious upheaval when my son was entering his teens, which I'm sure added to his already awkward introverted nature. He resisted making new friends in 9th and 10th grade. But as a few friendships developed, he opened up and began trying to participate. He matured in many ways as he grew up, and along with that his friendships matured.

8 // TALKING WITH TEENS

There is one aspect of homeschooling high school that was a bit of a surprise to me. In some ways it probably falls under parenting more than homeschooling, but it is still very foundational to the homeschool high school experience, and so I want to talk about it here.

You know how when your kids are little, you pretty much tell them what to do, and they do it? Obviously they are sometimes more willing than other times, and training is a thing, and we don't get perfect obedience–but when they are younger, they either do or they don't, and there isn't a lot of conversation about it.

In the teen years, though, that changes. All of a sudden your kid wants to question just about everything you say to them, and actually doing what you tell them to becomes an exercise in negotiation.

For whatever reason, conversation and discussion become a much larger part of parenting in the teen years. It's not just about things you want them to do, it's about life questions and the weird kid on the team and why the sky is blue and what kind of car they want and boy/girl stuff and their stupid sister. EVERYTHING needs to be discussed. Ad nauseum.

I bring this up here because it's a good thing to know going in. When you are blindsided by it, like I was, then you miss some golden opportunities, because you actually go to bed instead of sitting down on theirs and asking them to elaborate.

Yes, just when you are starting to need an earlier bedtime due to age, LOL, your kids once again rob you of a good night's sleep. It happened when they were infants and needing to be fed, as toddlers wanting to be calmed from a bad dream or given a drink or taken to the bathroom before an accident could happen—and now as teens it becomes a thing again. If I had a dollar for each of the times I wanted to go to bed and had to stay up to talk with one of my teens, I'd go on a shopping spree.

The conversation may start about one thing, but it usually ranges over a wide variety of topics before they are done. All of their angst must be vented into the atmosphere, whether loudly or in tears or disguised as philosophy, and you get to be the sentient being that nods and hmmms and occasionally (but not too often) interjects parental wisdom or empathy—more often the latter. Yes, some teens are untalkative—but they still really do want someone to listen. It's just a little harder to pry it out of them.

Yes, teens have feelings. And they have opinions. And they just want to tell you what they did today or what they are excited about. A huge part of maintaining a good relationship with them is to take the time to hear what they have to say.

How does this relate to homeschooling? Because when you homeschool high school, then it becomes a topic for conversation, too. In myriads of ways. And it's important to realize that your days of picking curriculum by yourself and determining your kid's schedule for them and even telling them the best way to do their schoolwork are now at an end. ALL of this is up for negotiation, and you either adapt to this and go with it or you end up with a stone wall attitude from your teen and big-time frustration. I've been there, so I know whereof I speak.

Here's where I mention the caveat that every teen is different and yours may never be as awful as mine occasionally were and you might even be the perfect parent to have brought that about—so if this chapter doesn't apply to you, then feel free to skip it. Or you might have a teen who doesn't need to discuss everything and is totally willing to follow your guidance even now. I've yet to meet one of those, but if yours is like that, then maybe this chapter is not for you.

For the rest of us, and I feel like it's probably the majority, then let's talk about talking. With your teen. About homeschooling. This may be one of the most important chapters in the whole book, frankly, so I do hope you stick around.

When you thought about your WHY in the earlier chapter, was your relationship with your teen on your list of reasons to keep homeschooling through high school? I think for many of us, even if we don't specify that in writing, we are still wanting to forge bonds and deepen the ties that exist between ourselves and this person who now is much more autonomous. We want them to know we are there for them, that we love them. And we want to become friends with them, rather than just being the parent. The teen years are a transition time that can be tricky to navigate, but the end result we are hoping for is to have a friendship with our teen similar to that we have with, well, our friends.

I am here to say that cultivating conversation during the high school years is one of the best ways to achieve that. As I alluded to earlier, I didn't realize this with my older kids–and there are bridges that are now much less steady than I wished for. I hope to give you this information before you need it, or at least in time to make some course corrections, so that the bridges between you and your teen are strengthened. So that the friendship you want to share eventually comes about easily and naturally. So you don't have any regrets to look back on.

The thing is, it's tough to identify that what your teen really needs is to talk to you, when they are instead in the act of screaming at you or rebelling against what you said. We want to enforce our authority and MAKE them do whatever it is, especially now that they are kicking up a fuss about it.

When my kids were all little, there was a phase where they voluntarily said (in response to an order from me), "Yes, Mommy; we'd be happy to do that, Mommy, because we love you, Mommy." Yes, with all the repetition; and they were being somewhat facetious but still expressing a willingness to obey with a cheerful heart, which was what we all aim for, right? Needless to say I LOVED it.

But then the teen years hit–and I never heard that any more. I used to ask them what happened to it, and they would reply, "Mom, really?" As if it was ridiculous for me to expect it, and they couldn't believe they had ever said it in the first place.

Instead I would get "But Mom…" or "In just a minute…" (and the minute never came) or "Do I have to?" or my personal favorite, "I don't have time" (often as they are playing a video game). Or worse, if it was a sensitive subject: "Would you just get off my back?" or "I know, I know…" (heavy sigh, rolls eyes). Or "That's it; I'm outta here" (into room and slams door).

Half the time it was when they originally had asked me for help in the first place. Math problems are a definite spark-producer, y'all. You CANNOT know more than they do about how to do the problem. They don't know how to do it, but whatever you say is not the right way, either, according to them. They interrupt, they say they know that already, they refuse to show their work so you can understand where they went wrong, "Forget it, I'll figure it out by myself"–and there you are again, in an argument.

It is definitely EASIER to argue than to converse. And it's so satisfying in the short term, isn't it? LOL. But it won't create the relationship you want. And apologizing to a teen later is possibly one of the most humiliating things ever! It's better to handle things in such a way that you have nothing to apologize for–and that's accomplished through conversation.

Set the Stage with Little Things

Okay, so how to make conversation happen? Especially if you're already characterized more by arguing than by constructive communication?

First it's necessary to set the atmosphere. And if the atmosphere is already one of dissension and frustration, then this phase might be more difficult but is very necessary. You can't just all of a sudden start trying to have conversations about anything, much less homeschooling, when there are relationship problems that cause communication issues. You probably don't trust each other very much at this point. So I recommend a few baby steps to transform the air between you first, before aiming for any heart-to-hearts.

Here are a few things you can do to ease the tension a bit. Some of them are easier than others, LOL. All of them are my own suggestions, not "must do's"–pick and choose what will work for you. And if you already feel like the relationship is pretty good, then these things might make it even better.

1) Stop talking back to them. "Wait a minute, this doesn't sound right–it's they who are talking back to me!!" But then the very next thing we do is snap right back, am I right? (Or is that just me?!?) The point here is to NOT be drawn in. Whatever they say, just receive it calmly and respond with an even tone, or don't reply back at all. If you have to, walk out of the room. But whatever you do, don't respond in kind.

They are looking to us to diffuse their frustration, not add to it. All they know is that they are frustrated, and half the time they can't even identify why– but whatever you last said to them was the trigger that gave them the excuse to vent it. You're just the convenient punching bag. Don't take it personally– which for me is VERY hard to do, LOL. But it is necessary to remember that we are supposed to be the adults, here. If we can't control ourselves, how can we expect them to?

2) Maintain physical affection, even when you just want to rip their eyeballs out. A touch on the shoulder (even if they yank away), a quick rub on the back or ruffling their hair. Hugs before bedtime. Hugs when you first see them in the morning. Whatever you like, as long as it's something that is showing affection in a way that they won't take as teasing.

Sometimes you have to say, with a smile in your voice, "I am going to hug you, whether you want to or not right now, because I am your parent and I love you." And then just give them as warm a hug as you can, even if it's short, even if they stand there like a brick wall. This IS registering in their little heart of hearts, even if they refuse to show it on the outside. And over time this helps, in my own non-psychologist-nor-therapist-nor-do-I-play-one-on-TV opinion.

3) Start smiling at them. Smile when you talk to them, smile at them from across the room, smile when you first see them after a time away. Show that you are glad they are there. Again, this registers, even if you think that they think you are being really stupid or look at you funny and say, "what?" as if you are truly ARE being stupid. You are NOT being stupid. You are reaching out to their heart; you are helping them like themselves more; you are building bridges. Tiny ones, but still.

4) Occasionally stop as you pass the door to their bedroom, stick your head in, and say "Hey dude, how's it going?" or something similar. They may mumble "fine" and not even lift their head. Accept that and move on down the hallway. The aim is for a short interaction that still shows you are thinking about them and are interested in them. We are water dripping on the stone... which will eventually make an impression.

5) If they are sitting out in a common area, find a book or something to do with your hands and go sit in the same room with them. No need to converse at this time, just sit there and do your own thing. Forget the idea of "quality time" with all of its pressures to do wonderful things with fantastic communication–just spend some time, any time, in the same room. If they are watching a movie, sit down and watch it with them, whether you are interested in it or not. You don't have to ask them questions about it or try to understand it while the movie is playing–in my house that would be VERY annoying to any one of us, LOL–just be there. Maybe later you can ask a question about a plot point that you weren't clear on, which would be a great way to–you guessed it–start a conversation.

6) Make them breakfast or lunch. As our kids get older, we tend to let them fend for themselves more. But it's my firm belief that food is a means of ministry–so get your teen's attention and ask them if they want some of what you're making for yourself. Or surprise them by taking their favorite sandwich to their room right before they would normally come out to eat. Don't expect thanks, just do it. Don't even expect them to eat it, LOL. The gesture is enough at this point.

Make cookies. Buy ice cream and offer it before bedtime. Make sure the pantry is stocked with some of their favorite snacks. Put a granola bar in their hand as they head out the door. Drop a Hershey's nugget in their lap as you walk by, or shout "heads up" from across the room and then toss it at them, whether they look up or not. LOL.

Food builds bridges. It just does.

7) When you are together in the car, let them run the music. GASP! This one can be headache-inducing, LOL. But it's so worth it. You can request a suitable volume level, but let them choose the songs or the station. You might even find that you like their selections! I used to think current pop was a waste of time until I started listening to what my kids were listening to. Now I often choose it, even when it's just me in the car! My son likes some sort of electric mayhem stuff, which is actually fairly musically complicated. It's not my choice yet, but he gets so enthusiastic, and it's a view into who he is.

Music is important to teens. Don't you remember that? Join them in it. Without criticism, LOL. That would defeat the purpose and set you back further than you were before. Don't go there; just trust me on this one.

8) Catch them being successful. And tell them about it, even if it's stupid. "Dude, thanks for picking your towel up off the bathroom floor! Way to go!" Yes, the towel should not be laying on the floor; the kid should be old enough to do that regularly just out of courtesy–but teens often don't think that way. They are pretty self-oriented, and it's lots easier to leave the towel on the floor in everyone's way.

Slight rabbit trail: I've said it before and I'll say it again–sometimes it seems like all the training you did when they were young goes completely out the door when they hit about 12 or 13. They act like you never taught them any kind of proper behavior at all. It can be SO frustrating! But again, baby steps.

OK, back to catching them doing good things: The point is to praise them when and as often as you can. Look for things to praise them about. Little things and big things.

Every teen does some things really well or has moments of behavioral brilliance. Notice those, and tell them you noticed. Not in a backhanded way, "Wow, thanks for FINALLY putting the car keys away!" LOL. Rather, "I found the car keys right where I needed them. Thanks, buddy!"

Again, don't expect a great response. Again, we are water dripping on stone. Again, make it short and sweet. Again, baby steps.

9) This one's a biggie: If they come to you for anything at all, STOP WHAT YOU ARE DOING and give them your full attention. I am here to tell you that it is SO tempting not to do this. But do it anyway. Turn the burners down, close the laptop cover, put the bookmarker at the page, turn off the vacuum cleaner. Look them in the eyes, listen to them, and answer them appropriately.

These teens are not small children any more. They aren't puppies. They have feelings, STRONG feelings, that are easily hurt by even the smallest things. You don't ever want to hear them say, "You never have time for me when I need you." "You don't pay any attention to me." "You won't listen to me." Even if you have done ALL of the above things for the last six months, not giving them your attention when they come to you one time can make them feel like you NEVER do. I know it's not reasonable or logical–we're talking about teens, here, remember? LOL.

Your relationship with them is more important than whatever you could possibly be doing at the moment–unless it's talking with your spouse. That might be the one exception. The relationship with the spouse DOES trump the relationship with the kids. Sometimes we forget that, but it's actually healthier that way for our kids. They actually PREFER that they be placed behind our spouse in the priority order, although they would probably never admit it or maybe even understand it.

But if it's anything else you're doing, then try as often as is earthly possible to put the teen first. If they want to talk with you, then now is the time. You might not have the opportunity later.

I know that often they want to talk about trivial stuff. They want to explain to you how they just won that exciting video game. They want to complain about how their sibling makes too much noise in the room next to theirs. They can't find their left shoe, and it's all someone else's fault. Sometimes you just want to tell them to get lost and leave you alone.

But here's the thing: Being available for them now sets the stage for them to come to you later, when there are big life issues that they are working their way through. When they are off at college and the girl across the hall tries to kill herself. When they damage the car late at night trying to get to a friend who has gotten herself into a bad situation. When they need advice about this guy who is interested in them. When they just want to hear a voice that they know will be supportive and encouraging, because they've been facing a lot of tough things lately.

Try as much as you can to be available NOW, so that they will feel free to come to you LATER. So they will WANT to come to you later. Each kid is different, and some are more self-sufficient while others want to tell you everything they're thinking—but in either case, I've learned (sometimes the hard way) that it's best in the long run not to shut down the opportunities that arise in the everyday.

10) Try as hard as you can not to overly criticise. Try to guide, not tell. You are more of a coach now, not the autocratic parent of a small child. Listing everything they did wrong or how their thinking is completely skewed is not a recipe for building bridges, LOL. Of course they are not doing everything "right,"—but find what is praiseworthy and mention it first.

I do believe there is room for CONSTRUCTIVE criticism, but with teens, I believe it needs to be very carefully worded. Teens, as noted before, are easily offended and will tend to put up walls without much provocation. You have to tread carefully.

I didn't always do this, y'all. And I still often don't, because I'm caught up in my own frustration and don't want to filter my response. That is not good adulting, is all I can say about it. Again, we need to be the ones in control, or how can we expect them to be?

Be an encourager. To "encourage" means to en-courage, to put courage into someone. Don't rip your teen down, instead build them up. Focus on what is being learned, even if it's happening the hard way. Focus on how you're there with them through everything and that you love them, regardless of how they've messed up. Tell them your own stupid mistake stories.

Being positive with all the little things they bring to you makes it a lot easier to do so with the big ones. Develop the habit of creating positivity, and you'll find it there to use when all you want to do is let them have it.

All of these things set the stage for a better relationship with your teen. But of course this won't happen overnight. If walls have been up for awhile, it will take awhile to bring them back down. Be patient, and just keep doing as much as you can to show them that you want to be sensitive to them and hear what they have to say, that you love them and even LIKE them.

Let your teens believe that you really do like who they are. Remember that their poor behavior now is a reflection of confusion and frustration, not necessarily of stupidity or irresponsibility. I mean, sometimes we do feel like we don't like them–I think that's normal in families, LOL. But we need to remember that's something that we feel in the moment, not long term. Don't be short-sighted, like they are. Act now with the lifelong relationship in mind, and try not to do or say anything you'll regret later.

BUT OF COURSE YOU WILL. Parenting is full of regrets. You will make mistakes, sometimes really big ones. Hopefully not as big as mine, since I'm giving you the hard-fought fruits of my mistake-filled labor, LOL.

When that happens, own it. Be an example to your teen of what it means to realize you've done or said something that you want to take back. Apologize sincerely, without excuses that reflect back on them for being the cause of your poor behavior. You chose your words/actions, so take full responsibility for them.

A friend of mine has a saying: "What's in the well will come up in the bucket, no matter what or who is pulling on the chain." We can't blame others for our own poor behavior. It was in us, and it came out. Own it.

They may not respond very well to your apology. That's OK; don't take it personally. Especially if you're not in the habit of doing this, your teen probably just won't know HOW to respond. But even if you've been great about acknowledging when you mess up, they can still be poopers about accepting apologies well. They love to hold onto their hurt. Didn't you, when you were that age?

WHY AM I BRINGING UP ALL THIS PARENTING STUFF WHEN THIS IS A HOMESCHOOL BOOK???

Because I think the relationship with your teen is one of the foundations of a successful homeschool high school experience. And being able to converse with your teen productively and well is going to make the whole thing a better experience for both of you. There is a lot to talk about!

One last thing about conversation in general before moving specifically to conversation about homeschooling–I've heard that there is a difference between how boys communicate and how girls communicate. With my kids, one boy and four girls, this isn't necessarily true, but since it may be true for you, I bring it up in case it might be helpful.

Here's what I've heard–I've heard that boys will communicate more readily side-by-side, while girls prefer face-to-face. What this means is that boys don't want the pressure of eye contact and having to reply immediately–they would rather be doing something together, side by side, at the same time as having a conversation. This is how guys communicate with each other, apparently (although what do I know about this, not being one, right?).

Girls, though, want to drop everything and talk. They want to be face-to-face with lots of eye contact and nothing else going on.

I do know this is true for me and my husband. My husband wants to talk deep stuff while we're driving down the road, and all I want him to do is stop the car right now so we can face each other and give full attention to the conversation. Or he wants to talk when we're getting ready to go somewhere, when I am trying to concentrate on doing my hair and makeup. Aargh.

With my kids, though, it's another story. My son, surprisingly, is totally into a one-on-one heart-to-heart while we are both perched on the bed in his room. It will range over a multitude of subjects, some difficult, some easier.

And I have a daughter who is actually hesitant to talk much at all about the deep stuff, and it will only occur after we've already been together in the car for awhile–and then we might get somewhere (other than our physical destination, LOL).

So obviously this depends on your kid; there are exceptions to everything, right? But I thought it might help, and it's certainly worth a try to find something to do together with your son before expecting him to open up. Or to take your daughter out to breaky, just you two, and then start asking some probing questions.

Conversing about Homeschooling

After we've broken the ice for a more open relationship with our teen, it becomes easier to talk about all the issues that come up as we are homeschooling with them. They want a say in things at this point; they don't want to be told what to study (or how!) any more. I do recommend conferring with your teen about course requirements, curriculum choices, schedule, etc. I think they should have some input in the decisions that are made about how to get through the high school years in your homeschool. You want your teen on board, motivated to do what they need to do to graduate. Letting them tell you what they want and don't want as you are doing the planning goes a long way towards making that happen.

It's not a guarantee, though, so don't expect that just because you purchase the exact course and curriculum that your teen said they wanted means that they will happily do it each and every day and get an A because they just loved it so much. Nope, LOL. But they do have feelings and opinions about what they want to learn and how they want to do it. Give some consideration to those, and you'll find this whole endeavor goes that much more smoothly.

Does that mean they get to call all the shots? Nope again. You are still the parent; you still have the long-range experience. You also know your teen better than they know themselves, so you are more aware of what will work for them and what won't. You can still make decisions that they disagree with; you still have the final say.

Just try not to pull the parent card any more often than necessary. One example of when I did use it was what I shared earlier, about when we learned the hard way with #1 that she could have gotten thousands more in scholarship money with just a point or two increase of her ACT score. She had told me after the first time taking it that she never wanted to do that again, and I acquiesced. Well, not with anyone else, LOL. They have all been TOLD by me that they WILL take the test at least twice.

Another thing that we pulled the parent card about was continuing complaints about wanting to go to public school. We did make it very clear from the beginning that we were in this homeschooling thing through graduation, and repetitive conversations about quitting would not be on the table.

As we've discussed in the WHY chapter, you may need to explain to your teen your reasons for deciding to homeschool high school, and so it's important to have them thought out and be prepared to express them when necessary. But that doesn't mean the teen can expect you to do so every other week when they are frustrated. We didn't tolerate that. At times we just said something to the effect of, "Yo, this is how it is, and it's not going to change. It is in your best interests to adapt and deal. End of story."

This might be the ONE other situation that you can be unavailable for when your kid wants to talk, LOL. There are only so many times you can go around any given merry-go-round, and the "I hate homeschooling, I want to go to public school" whine is only acceptable on an infrequent basis. By definition, a teen has no real clue what life is all about. They haven't lived long enough to understand the ramifications of what they are asking for. YOU DO, and YOU HAVE.

But pulling the parent card in this instance doesn't have to be fraught with tension. You can say, "We love you, and we believe we know what will be best for you over the long haul. You don't have to agree with us, but you do need to abide by our decision in this matter. It truly is made based on our own years of experience, and our knowledge of who you are. Please trust us." Be gentle–but firm.

Is this a fail-proof method of confronting this issue? Of course not, because we are still talking about teens, remember, who have the ability to turn even the most loving moment into a trip into Mordor. But again I recommend the self-control plan, the loving approach, no matter how it is received.

This may have been easier for us, since we had been homeschooling since before our oldest started kindergarten, always with the plan of doing so all the way through high school. Our kids already knew this was the way it was and that whatever they said wasn't going to change it. So we haven't had much backlash about this, thankfully. Our kids bring it up more from curiosity–"I wonder what public school is like?"–than from a sincere hope to go there.

But it would be difficult to successfully homeschool high school with a teen who refuses to let that dog lie. Yes, they can get hold of an idea and wring it to death, and then wring it some more–but my recommendation is to as calmly as possible make it clear that thoughts of public school will not be entertained.

Otherwise, it is my belief that you won't make it all the way to the end. If public or private school is always an out, then when the frustrations of homeschooling high school rear their heads–and they will, because while it's wonderful it can also be difficult sometimes–then it will seem easier to just quit and take them to school after all.

Just like marriage is a commitment that you stick to no matter what, homeschooling high school should seem that way also, in my opinion. There shouldn't be the option to quit. Once you're in, you need to be all in, for the long haul, through sickness and health, from freshman to senior, etc. LOL. Because I think that kind of commitment will be one of the key factors in your success.

If your teen needs to talk about it a couple times a year, that's one thing. If they want to bring it up a couple times a month–don't entertain that. We parents have to be the leaders, and sometimes that means doing things that the underlings don't like. We are not out to win a popularity contest but to parent our kids the best way we know how. And that may mean going against their wishes in the homeschool vs. public/private school debate. So be it.

When you take the time to build and maintain a solid relationship with your teen, including them in decisions that affect them and speaking to them with respect and self-control, the whole homeschool high school endeavor becomes much more doable. Then you can discuss the things that aren't working well and brainstorm ways to fix them–together. And the relationship that started before they were even born can continue to grow as they do, and you'll find that it's a wonderful thing to have adult children who are also your FRIENDS. It's possible, though you may have trouble believing it when you're in the trenches of teen warfare. Hang in there!

Jill:

The biggest surprise about parenting teens was that I would be ready for it when the time came. I never knew how to talk to teens till I had them. Now it's no problem.

Also, parents only talk among themselves about super genius kids or teen attitudes. I try to say what a joy it is to have budding adults and seek to enjoy them as our relationships morph into the advisor role more than the authority role.

The most important thing for keeping relationships with them solid was recognizing I don't have control over their hearts. Attempting to control a teen-age heart in a way only God can pushes a child away. So a minimal amount of needful rules, a kind tongue, excessive patience and a deep love for who God has made them to be individually provide the soil for a flourishing relationship.

Also, not punishing kids in a "repay evil for evil" manner. For example–

you hurt me, teenager, with your choice so I'm going to make sure I hurt you with my response or a painful punishment.

I have caught myself with these thoughts at times and have been thankful for the Lord's restraining hand and my husband's wise leadership and am learning to not respond this way even in my thoughts now.

Angie:

What I know now is my son at age 14 is going to be significantly different than that son at 18 years old. The age comparison might be different for girls, but the lesson is the same. Don't assume you know who your child will be when they are still just children. They might be six feet tall and sound like a grown man, but they are still young and immature and likely will change and mature beyond your expectations.

9 // CONCLUSION

Phew, we've covered a LOT of ground! Are you still with me?

I hope that now you're feeling much better about homeschooling high school and that it is not as intimidating as it was before you started reading.

I hope you've gotten not just some practical ideas but also a renewed sense of what you're doing and where you're going, a foundation on which to build.

Most of all, I hope you have established a mindset of realistic expectations shored up by reasonable standards and the willingness to flex when (not if!) it becomes necessary.

As Sarah Mackenzie says in Teaching from Rest (p. 63), "When you are performing mommy triage–that is, when you have a crisis moment and you have to figure out which fire to put out first–always choose your child… Don't damage the relationship over something so trivial as an algebra problem."

We will have choices each and every day as we homeschool high school. Choices about curriculum, assignments, schedules, what to focus on, and what to let go. But all of it–ALL of it–is less important than that teen whom we love so dearly that our chest literally aches. Don't hold so fast to your way of doing things that you lose your teen's heart in the process. Don't keep your standards so high that your kid despairs of ever pleasing you. Don't plan their life for them or shield them from stumbling or hover over them or hinder their independence.

All of these things are tendencies for the homeschool mom more so than the public or private school mom, I think, because we see our kids' lives in minute detail from sunup to sundown. Public school kids make all sorts of decisions throughout the day that mom never knows about. While we're not necessarily trying to emulate that, we need to appreciate that our teens have thoughts and opinions and wishes and dreams–and we are in the unique position to watch as they figure all of these out. Handle with care, and hold your own plans and ideas and wishes for them loosely.

When you homeschool high school, you have a front row seat as your kid matures from awkward tween to fascinating young adult. How do you want to look back on that time? While we will all have regrets–some little, some big–my wish for you is that you are able to savor the moments, embrace the changes, and ultimately enjoy the ride.

HUGS!!

ABOUT THE AUTHOR

Ann has been homeschooling for 19+ years and has graduated four children (one more to go). She believes that EVERY mom can confidently, competently—and even contentedly—provide the complete high school education that her teen needs.

Ann's website, *AnnieandEverything.com*, offers information, resources, and virtual hugs to help homeschool moms do just that. Ann has also written *Cure the Fear of Homeschooling High School: A Step-by-Step Handbook for Research & Planning*.

She and her family, including two dogs and three cats, live in rural Missouri.

Made in the USA
Columbia, SC
26 May 2020